Ben Stacy Jerrik (Ed.)

Computer Professionals for Social Responsibility

Ben Stacy Jerrik (Ed.)

Computer Professionals for Social Responsibility

Electronic Privacy Information Center, Computers, Freedom and Privacy Conference

Part Press

Contents

Articles

References

Computer_Professionals_for_Social_Responsibility

Computer Professionals for Social Responsibility	
Abbreviation	CPSR
Motto	Technology is driving the future... it is up to us to do the steering
Formation	1983
Type	NGO
Purpose/focus	impacts of computer technology on society
Headquarters	Seattle, Washington
Website	cpsr.org [1]

Computer Professionals for Social Responsibility (CPSR) is a global organization promoting the responsible use of computer technology. CPSR was incorporated [2] in 1983 (following discussions and organizing that began in 1981). It educates policymakers and the public on a wide range of issues. CPSR has incubated numerous projects such as Privaterra, the Public Sphere Project [3], EPIC (the Electronic Privacy Information Center), the 21st Century Project, the Civil Society Project, and the CFP (Computers, Freedom and Privacy) Conference. Originally founded by U.S. computer scientists at Stanford University and Xerox PARC, CPSR now has members in over 30 countries on six continents. CPSR is a non-profit 501.c.3 organization registered in California.

When CPSR was first established it was concerned solely about the use of computers in warfare. This initially was focused on the Strategic Computing Initiative, a US Defense project to use artificial intelligence in military systems, but added opposition to the Strategic Defense Initiative (SDI) shortly after the program was announced. The Boston chapter helped organize a debate related to the software reliability of SDI systems which drew national attention ("Software Seen as Obstacle in Developing 'Star Wars', Philip M. Boffey, (New York Times, September 16, 1986) to these issues. Later, workplace issues, privacy, and community networks were added to CPSR's agenda.

CPSR was originally a chapter-based organization and had chapters in Palo Alto, Boston, Seattle, Austin, Washington, DC, Portland (Oregon) and other US locations as well as a variety of international chapters including Peru and Spain. The chapters often developed innovative projects including a slide show about the dangers of launch on warning (Boston chapter) and the Seattle Community Network [4] (Seattle chapter).

CPSR sponsored two conferences: the Participatory Design Conferences which is held biennially (the most recent, the 11th is being held in Sydney, Australia) and the Directions and Implications of Advanced Computing (DIAC) symposium series which was launched in 1987 in Seattle. The DIAC symposia have been convened roughly every other year since that time (most recently in October , 2010 in Prato Italy in conjunction with the Community Information Research Network (CIRN) annual conference. Four books (*Directions and Implications of Advanced Computing*; *Reinventing Technology, Rediscovering Community*; *Community Practice in the Network Society*; and *Shaping the Network Society*) and two special sections in the Communications of the ACM ("Social Responsibility" and "Social Computing") resulted from the DIAC symposia.

CPSR awards the Norbert Wiener Award for Social and Professional Responsibility. Some notable recipients include David Parnas, Joseph Weizenbaum, Kristen Nygaard, Barbara Simons, Antonia Stone, Peter G. Neumann, Marc Rotenberg, Mitch Kapor, and Douglas Engelbart.

External links

- Computer Professionals for Social Responsibility [5]
- Documentary film about Norbert Wiener Award winner, Joseph Weizenbaum ("Weizenbaum. Rebel at Work.") [6]
- Computer Professionals for Social Responsibility Records, 1983-1991. [7] Charles Babbage Institute, University of Minnesota.
- Oral history interview with Severo Ornstein and Laura Gould [8], Charles Babbage Institute, University of Minnesota. Oral history interview by Bruce Bruemmer, 1994, discussing the formation and activities of Computer Professionals for Social Responsibility.

References

[1] http://www.cpsr.org
[2] http://www.cpsr.org/about/history
[3] http://www.publicsphereproject.org/
[4] http://www.scn.org
[5] http://www.cpsr.org/
[6] http://www.ilmarefilm.org/W_E_1.htm
[7] http://purl.umn.edu/40803
[8] http://purl.umn.edu/107336

Electronic_Privacy_Information_Center

Electronic Privacy Information Center (**EPIC**) is a public interest research group in Washington, D.C. It was established in 1994 to focus public attention on emerging civil liberties issues and to protect privacy, the First Amendment, and constitutional values in the information age. EPIC pursues a wide range of activities, including privacy research, public education, conferences, litigation, publications, and advocacy.

EPIC maintains web sites (epic.org [1] and privacy.org [2]) and publishes the online EPIC Alert [3] every two weeks with information about emerging privacy and civil liberties issues. EPIC also publishes *Privacy and Human Rights, Litigation Under the Federal Open Government Laws, The Public Voice WSIS Sourcebook, The Privacy Law Sourcebook,* and *The Consumer Law Sourcebook.* EPIC litigates high-profile privacy, First Amendment, and Freedom of Information Act cases. EPIC advocates for strong privacy safeguards.

In addition to maintaining privacy.org, EPIC also coordinates the Public Voice coalition [4], and the Privacy Coalition [5]. EPIC also established the National Committee on Voting Integrity [6].

Background

EPIC was founded in 1994 by David Banisar, Marc Rotenberg, and David Sobel [7], as a joint project of the Fund for Constitutional Government and Computer Professionals for Social Responsibility. Early on, the organization focused on government surveillance and cryptography issues, such as the Clipper Chip and the Communications Assistance for Law Enforcement Act, or CALEA. After becoming an independent non-profit organization in November 2000, EPIC has continued to work on governmental issues: surveillance; transparency, using the Freedom of Information Act to publicize documents; and the security, verifiability, and privacy of electronic voting. It has also taken up the growing number of consumer privacy issues, such as identity theft, phone record security, medical record privacy,

and commercial data mining. In 1997 Wayne Madsen, now an investigative journalist on international security issues and counterterrorism, joined EPIC as a senior fellow, leaving in 2005[8]

Organizational structure

EPIC is registered as a non-profit Public Charity, and receives most of its funding from organizational and individual contributors, as well as through grants and the sale of its publications.

Criticisms

EPIC has been criticized by both opponents and supporters for what are seen as its extreme positions on privacy issues. The June 1995 issue of *Wired*[9] quoted a member of the Electronic Frontier Foundation as saying that EPIC "made everybody else at the table look moderate. It's the old good-cop-bad-cop routine."

Publications

EPIC maintains and publishes its newsletter, the EPIC Alert, every two weeks.

EPIC also publishes several books on privacy and open government, including *Privacy and Human Rights, Litigation Under the Federal Open Government Laws, Filters and Freedom, The Public Voice WSIS Sourcebook, The Privacy Law Sourcebook,* and *The Consumer Law Sourcebook.*

Other publications include reports on internet privacy for web surfers, an analysis of industry self-regulation, and how Internet filtering software can block innocuous sites.

EPIC also maintains privacy.org, and the Privacy Coalition. In addition, EPIC coordinates the Public Voice coalition, launched in 1996 to promote public and NGO participation in decisions concerning the future of the Internet, as well as the National Committee for Voting Integrity, which was established to promote voter-verified balloting and to preserve privacy protections for elections in the United States.

Historical timeline

- **February 2012**: EPIC filed a complaint with the FTC about Google's new consolidated Privacy Policy saying it allowed advertising companies easier access to the data the user viewed in Google services.
- **March 2009**: EPIC filed a complaint with the Federal Trade Commission asking it to examine the privacy protections in Google's cloud computing applications including Picasa, Google Docs and Gmail after an error exposed users' documents publicly without permission.[10]
- **April 2007**: EPIC, along with the Center for Digital Democracy and U.S. PIRG, filed a complaint[11] with the Federal Trade Commission, urging the Commission to open an investigation into the proposed acquisition of DoubleClick by Google. The groups urged the FTC to assess the ability of Google to record, analyze, track, and profile the activities of Internet users with data that is both personally identifiable and data that is not personally identifiable. The groups further urged the FTC to require Google to publicly present a plan to comply with well-established government and industry privacy standards such as the OECD Privacy Guidelines. Pending the resolution of these and other issues, EPIC encouraged the FTC to halt the acquisition.
- **April 2007**: In response to a petition filed by EPIC, the Federal Communications Commission issued rules to protect the privacy of consumers' telephone records.
- **March 2007**: In testimony[12] before the House Committee on Energy and Commerce, EPIC Executive Director Marc Rotenberg expressed support for H.R. 936, the Prevention of Fraudulent Access to Phone Records Act.

- **February 2007**: In testimony[13] before the House Committee on Energy and Commerce, EPIC staff counsel Allison Knight testified in support of the Truth in Caller ID Act of 2007.
- **November 2006**: EPIC joined with other organizations in urging the Supreme Court to review Gilmore v. Gonzales. The case concerns a secret rule that allows airport personnel to require travelers in the United States to produce identification. EPIC's brief said that the secret agency rule "offends the Constitution and implicates the rights of millions of American travelers who are presently subject to arbitrary and unaccountable governmental authority."
- **May 2006**: EPIC Executive Director Marc Rotenberg testified[14] at a hearing before the House Subcommittee on Telecommunications and the Internet on the Truth in Caller ID Act of 2006, a bill that would outlaw "spoofing" telephone calls.
- **April 2006**: EPIC filed a friend of the court brief[15] in Peterson v. NTIA supporting the rights of .US domain name holders not to publish their personal information on the Internet. In 2005, the Department of Commerce, which administers the .US domain, banned users from using proxy services that would protect privacy.
- **February 2006**: In testimony[16] before the Senate Committee on Commerce, Science and Transportation, EPIC Executive Director Marc Rotenberg called for a ban on the sale of communications records, as well as a ban on "pretexting," the practice of using false pretenses to trick a company into releasing personal information.
- **February 2006**: In a Freedom of Information Act complaint[17] filed in federal court, EPIC sought the release of National Security Agency documents detailing the Administration's warrantless domestic surveillance program.
- **February 2006**: EPIC Executive Director Marc Rotenberg testified[18] before the House Committee on Energy and Commerce on the sale of personal phone records. EPIC called for laws that would ban pretexting (a technique used by data brokers to obtain personal information), as well as enhanced security procedures, and restrictions on the collection of customer data.
- **January 2006**: The Federal Trade Commission announced a settlement with data broker Choicepoint, under which the company had to pay $10 million to the Commission and $5 million to redress consumer harms. It was the largest civil penalty in FTC history. EPIC had filed a complaint with the Federal Trade Commission in December 2004 urging the agency to investigate the compilation and sale of personal dossiers by data brokers such as ChoicePoint.
- **January 2006**: EPIC filed a Freedom of Information Act lawsuit[19] against the Justice Department, asking a federal court to order the disclosure of information about the Administration's warrantless domestic surveillance program within 20 days.
- **January 2006**: EPIC filed suit[20] in federal court against the Justice Department for reports of possible misconduct submitted by the FBI to the Intelligence Oversight Board.
- **November 2005**: EPIC testified before the House Homeland Security Committee and warned that the new plan for passenger screening was still flawed. EPIC recommended that the program not go forward until its problems were fixed.
- **November 2005**: Judge Gladys Kessler ordered the FBI to publicly release or account for 1,500 pages responsive to EPIC's Freedom of Information Act request every fifteen days.
- **October 2005**: Documents obtained by EPIC under the Freedom of Information Act described thirteen cases of possible FBI misconduct in intelligence investigations.
- **October 2005**: EPIC and Patient Privacy Rights launched a joint campaign to strengthen protections for patients' medical information.
- **October 2005**: EPIC filed an amicus brief in a federal case that raised the question of whether the police may coerce a person to provide a DNA sample. EPIC's brief, which provided detailed information on the many problems with DNA dragnets, argued that very clear guidelines must be established before the police may engage in this practice.
- **October 2005**: EPIC led a campaign of more than 100 organizations that urged Secretary of Defense Donald Rumsfeld to end the "Joint Advertising and Market Research Studies" Recruiting Database.

- **August 2005**: EPIC petitioned[21] the Federal Communications Commission to initiate a rulemaking to enhance security safeguards for individuals' calling records. The petition follows a complaint[22] concerning the illegal sale of personal information obtained from telephone carriers, and an updated filing[23] where EPIC identified 40 websites that openly offer to obtain calling records without the knowledge and consent of the account holder.
- **August 2005**: EPIC and a coalition of open government organizations filed an amicus brief[24] in Gonzales v. Doe, a lawsuit concerning the FBI's authority to issue national security letters without judicial approval and under a permanent gag order that bans the recipient from telling anyone about the demand.
- **July 2005**: EPIC testified before the House Commerce Subcommittee on Consumer Protection. EPIC urged Congress to pass strong data security legislation that includes privacy protections for use of personal information.
- **July 2005**: EPIC testified before the Senate Foreign Relations Committee in opposition to the ratification of the Council of Europe Convention on Cybercrime. EPIC urged the Senate to oppose ratification because of the convention's sweeping expansion of law enforcement authority, the lack of legal safeguards, and the impact on U.S. Constitutional rights.
- **May 2005**: EPIC testified before the House Judiciary Committee on one of several proposals before Congress to impose new employment verification requirements on those wishing to work within the U.S. The legislation would require all workers to obtain a Social Security Number card that would be machine-readable, and would also empower the Department of Homeland Security to determine employment eligibility of those seeking employment. EPIC opposed the creation of this new employment verification system.
- **April 2005**: EPIC filed a complaint[25] asking a federal court to force the FBI to disclose information about its use of expanded investigative authority granted by sunsetting provisions of the USA PATRIOT Act. The agency had agreed[26] to quickly process EPIC's Freedom of Information Act request[27] for the data, but had not complied with the timeline for even a standard FOIA request.
- **March 2005**: EPIC urged lawmakers to regulate Choicepoint and other data brokers in testimony before the House Commerce Subcommittee on Consumer Protection. EPIC testified that there is too much secrecy and too little accountability in the business dealings of data brokers, and that Choicepoint's selling of customer information to identity thieves underscored the need for federal regulation of the information broker industry.
- **January 2005**: EPIC learned through Freedom of Information Act litigation that the FBI had obtained 257.5 million Passenger Name Records following 9/11, and that the Bureau has permanently incorporated the travel details of tens of millions of innocent people into its law enforcement databases.

References

[1] http://www.epic.org/

[2] http://www.privacy.org/

[3] http://www.epic.org/alert/

[4] http://www.thepublicvoice.org/

[5] http://www.privacycoalition.org/

[6] http://www.votingintergrity.org/

[7] https://www.eff.org/about/staff/david-sobel

[8] Wayne Madsen Jaded Tasks, page ix (http://www.scribd.com/doc/8470565/Jaded-Tasks)

[9] "3.06: Electric Word" (http://www.wired.com/wired/archive/3.06/eword.html). Wired.com. January 4, 2009. . Retrieved August 12, 2010.

[10] 12:09 p.m. Today12:09 p.m. Aug. 11, 2010. "Privacy group asks FTC to investigate Google reliability" (http://www.marketwatch.com/news/story/Privacy-group-asks-FTC-investigate/story.aspx?guid={C6CA7820-1512-4CC5-B78E-1173138182E3}). MarketWatch. . Retrieved August 12, 2010.

[11] http://epic.org/privacy/ftc/google/epic_complaint.pdf

[12] http://www.epic.org/privacy/iei/roten_hcom0307.pdf

[13] http://www.epic.org/privacy/iei/hr251test.pdf

[14] http://www.epic.org/privacy/iei/hr5126test.pdf

[15] http://www.epic.org/privacy/peterson/epic_peterson_amicus.pdf

[16] "EPIC Testimony on Protecting Consumers' Phone Records, February 8, 2006" (http://epic.org/privacy/iei/sencomtest2806.html). Epic.org. . Retrieved August 12, 2010.

[17] http://epic.org/privacy/nsa/amended_complaint.pdf

[18] "Microsoft Word - pretext_testimony.doc" (http://epic.org/privacy/iei/pretext_testimony.pdf) (PDF). . Retrieved August 12, 2010.

[19] http://epic.org/privacy/nsa/complaint_doj.pdf

[20] http://epic.org/privacy/terrorism/iob_complaint.pdf

[21] "CPNI" (http://epic.org/privacy/iei/cpnipet.html). EPIC. . Retrieved August 12, 2010.

[22] "EPIC Online Investigation Complaint" (http://epic.org/privacy/iei/ftccomplaint.html). Epic.org. . Retrieved August 12, 2010.

[23] "EPIC Update to the Federal Trade Commission on Online Data Brokers and CPNI" (http://epic.org/privacy/iei/ftcupdate.html).
       Epic.org. . Retrieved August 12, 2010.

[24] "Microsoft Word - FINAL NSL Amicus Brief.doc" (http://epic.org/open_gov/nsl/secrecy_amicus.pdf) (PDF). . Retrieved August 12,
       2010.

[25] http://www.epic.org/privacy/terrorism/usapatriot/sunset_complaint.pdf

[26] http://www.epic.org/privacy/terrorism/usapatriot/sunset_reply.pdf

[27] http://www.epic.org/privacy/terrorism/usapatriot/sunset_request.pdf

External links

- Official website (http://epic.org/)

Computers,_Freedom_and_Privacy_Conference

The **Computers, Freedom and Privacy Conference** (or **CFP**, or the **Conference on Computers, Freedom and Privacy**) is an annual academic conference held in the USA or Canada about the intersection of computer technology, freedom, and privacy issues. The conference founded in 1991, and since 2000, it has been organized under the aegis of the Association for Computing Machinery. It was also originally sponsored by CPSR.

The twenty-first annual CFP Conference in 2011, "Computers, Freedom, and Privacy: The Future is Now", will be held at the Georgetown Law Center in Washington, DC June 14-16. Among the questions and issues that will be explored are: What is social media's role in the charged democracy movement in the Middle East and North Africa; How can technology and social media support human rights, What is the impact of mobile personal computing technology on freedom and privacy? Are the courts, policy and decision makers ready to address freedom and privacy in a 24-7 connected world? Are our leaders techs savvy enough to make good legal and policy decisions regarding the deployment of smart grid, e-health records, the spread of consumer location based advertising? Cybersecurity, cloud computing, net neutrality, federated ID, ubiquitous surveillance: Are they passing fads or here to stay? [1]

The Fifteenth Conference on Computers, Freedom, and Privacy, which created this wiki page, was held in Seattle. The theme of this conference was equiveillance, the balance between surveillance and sousveillance. The equiveillance theme was reflected in the Opening Keynote Address, a panel discussion on equiveillance, and a pre-keynote sousveillance workshop, as well as a sousveillance performance.[2] In keeping with this theme, every conference attendee received a sousveillance system consisting of a "maybecamera" attached to each conference bag. Some of the 500 conference bags contained cameras transmitting live 24/7 video whereas others contained no camera, but merely

ACM CFP conference bags just after manufacture.

the familiar camera dome. A third category of conference bag included some with a subtle but visible flashing red light behind the dome. Not all of the wireless web cameras had flashing red lights, and some of the flashing red lights were dummy devices that did not transmit video. The bags that did transmit video also updated various video displays around the conference hall, visible to conference attendees.

References

[1] http://www.cfp.org/2011/wiki/index.php/Main_Page
[2] http://wearcam.org/cfp2005/

- Official site (http://www.cfp.org/)

PARC_(company)

Industry	R&D
Founded	1970
Headquarters	Palo Alto, California, USA
Parent	Xerox
Website	parc.com [1]

PARC (Palo Alto Research Center Incorporated), formerly **Xerox PARC**, is a research and development company in Palo Alto, California,[2] [3] [4] with a distinguished reputation for its contributions to information technology and hardware systems.

Founded in 1970 as a division of Xerox Corporation, PARC has been responsible for such well known and important developments as laser printing, Ethernet, the modern personal computer, graphical user interface (GUI), object-oriented programming, ubiquitous computing, amorphous silicon (a-Si) applications, and advancing very-large-scale-integration (VLSI) for semiconductors.

Incorporated as an independent but wholly owned subsidiary of Xerox in 2002, PARC now works with other commercial (major corporations, ventures, licensees) and government partners.

PARC entrance.

Xerox PARC old logo.

History

In 1969, Chief Scientist at Xerox Jack Goldman approached Dr. George Pake, a physicist specializing in nuclear magnetic resonance and provost of Washington University, about starting a second research center for the company.

Pake selected Palo Alto, California, as the site of what was to become known as PARC. While the 3,000 mile buffer between it and Xerox headquarters in Rochester, New York afforded scientists at the new lab great freedom to undertake their work, the distance also served as an impediment in persuading management of the promise of some of their greatest achievements.

PARC's West Coast location proved to be advantageous in the mid-1970s, when the lab was able to hire many employees of the nearby SRI Augmentation Research Center as that facility's funding from DARPA, NASA, and the U.S. Air Force began to diminish. Being situated on Stanford Research Park land leased from Stanford University [5] allowed Stanford graduate students to be involved in PARC research projects, and PARC scientists to collaborate with academic seminars and projects.

Much of PARC's early success in the computer field was under the leadership of its Computer Science Laboratory manager Bob Taylor, who guided the lab as associate manager from 1970–77 and as manager 1977–83.

PARC today

After three decades as a division of Xerox, PARC was transformed in 2002 into an independent, wholly owned subsidiary company dedicated to developing and maturing advances in science and business concepts with the support of commercial partners and clients.

Xerox remains the company's largest customer (50%), but PARC has numerous other corporate and venture clients in different fields of use than Xerox including: VMware, Fujitsu, Dai Nippon Printing Co., Ltd. (DNP), Samsung, NEC, SolFocus, Powerset, and many more.

PARC currently conducts research into "clean technology", user interface design, sensemaking, ubiquitous computing and context-aware systems, large-area electronics, and model-based control and optimization in embedded, intelligent systems.

Accomplishments

Xerox PARC has been the inventor and incubator of many elements of modern computing in the contemporary office work place:

- Laser printers,
- Computer-generated bitmap graphics
- The Graphical user interface, featuring windows and icons, operated with a mouse
- The WYSIWYG text editor
- InterPress, a resolution-independent graphical page-description language and the precursor to PostScript
- Ethernet as a local-area computer network
- Fully formed object-oriented programming in the Smalltalk programming language and integrated development environment.

The Alto

Most of these developments were included in the Alto, which added the now familiar SRI-developed mouse[6] unifying into a single model most aspects of now-standard personal computer use. The integration of Ethernet prompted the development of the PARC Universal Packet architecture, much like today's Internet.

The GUI

Xerox has been heavily criticized (particularly by business historians) for failing to properly commercialize and profitably exploit PARC's innovations. A favorite example is the GUI, initially developed at PARC for the Alto and then commercialized as the Xerox Star by the Xerox Systems Development Department. Although very significant in terms of its influence on future system design, it is deemed a failure because it only sold approximately 25,000 units. A small group from PARC led by David Liddle and Charles Irby formed Metaphor Computer Systems. They extended the Star desktop concept into an animated graphic and communicating office-automation model and sold the company to IBM.

Xerox Alto

Adoption by Apple

The first successful commercial GUI product was the Apple Macintosh, which was heavily inspired by PARC's work; Xerox was allowed to buy pre-IPO stock from Apple, in exchange for engineer visits and an understanding that Apple would create a GUI product[7] .

Much later, in the midst of the 1988-1994 Apple vs. Microsoft lawsuit, in which Apple accused Microsoft of violating its copyright by appropriating the use of the "look and feel" of the Apple Macintosh GUI, Xerox also sued Apple on similar grounds. The Xerox lawsuit was dismissed because the presiding judge dismissed most of Xerox's complaints as being inappropriate for a variety of legal reasons.[8] .

However, Apple's designs included quite a few concepts that were not part of (or were non-trivial advances to) the prototype developed at PARC. For example[7] :

- The mouse was not invented at PARC, but by Douglas Engelbart in 1963, Apple's mouse was an improvement on PARC's version.
- Unlike the Macintosh, PARC's prototype was incapable of any direct manipulation of widgets.
- Unlike the Macintosh, PARC's prototype did not feature Menu bars, or pull-down menu, nor the trash.
- Unlike the Macintosh, PARC's windows could not overlap each other.

Distinguished researchers

Among PARC's distinguished researchers were three Turing Award winners: Butler W. Lampson (1992), Alan Kay (2003), and Charles P. Thacker (2009). The ACM Software System Award recognized the Alto system in 1984, Smalltalk in 1987, InterLisp in 1992, and Remote Procedure Call in 1994. Lampson, Kay, Bob Taylor, and Charles P. Thacker received the National Academy of Engineering's prestigious Charles Stark Draper Prize in 2004 for their work on the Alto.

People associated with PARC

- Daniel G. Bobrow
- David Boggs
- Anita Borg
- John Seely Brown
- Stuart Card
- Robert Carr
- Ed Chi
- Elizabeth F. Churchill
- Lynn Conway
- Franklin C. Crow
- Pavel Curtis
- Steve Deering
- L Peter Deutsch
- Paul Dourish
- Clarence Ellis
- David Em
- William English
- David Eppstein
- Charles Geschke
- Adele Goldberg
- Jack Goldman
- Timothy A. Gonsalves
- Bill Gosper
- Rich Gossweiler
- Bruce Horn
- Bernardo Huberman
- Dan Ingalls
- Van Jacobson
- Natalie Jeremijenko
- Ronald Kaplan
- Alan Kay
- Martin Kay
- Gregor Kiczales
- Ralph Kimball
- Butler Lampson
- Cristina Lopes
- Andrew K. Ludwick
- David Maynard
- Edward M. McCreight
- Ralph Merkle
- Diana Merry
- Robert Metcalfe
- Jim Mitchell
- Thomas P. Moran
- James H. Morris
- Martin Newell
- Geoffrey Nunberg
- Severo Ornstein
- George Pake
- Randy Pausch
- Prasad Ram
- George G. Robertson
- Eric Schmidt
- Ronald V. Schmidt
- Scott Shenker
- John Shoch
- Charles Simonyi
- Brian Cantwell Smith
- Robert Spinrad
- Bob Sproull
- Gary Starkweather
- Bert Sutherland
- Robert Taylor
- Shang-Hua Teng
- Larry Tesler
- Chuck Thacker
- Bill Verplank
- John Warnock
- Mark Weiser
- Niklaus Wirth
- Frances Yao
- Annie Zaenen

Legacy

PARC's developments in information technology have had great long-term impact. Once the merits of interfaces and technology pioneered by PARC became widely known, they evolved into standards for much of the computing industry. Many advances were not equalled or surpassed for two decades, enormous timespans in the fast-paced high-tech world.

While there is some truth that Xerox management failed to see the potential of many of PARC's inventions, it is an over-simplification to generalize. The larger reality is that computing research was a relatively small part of PARC's operation. Its materials scientists pioneered LCD and optical disc technologies, others invented laser printing, each of which proved great successes when introduced to the business and consumer marketplaces.[9]

While not of the same order, the oft-overlooked work at PARC since the early 1980s includes advances in ubiquitous computing, aspect-oriented programming, and IPv6.

See also

- Xerox Daybreak (a.k.a. Xerox Windows 6085)
- GlobalView

References

[1] http://www.parc.com/

[2] " Contact (http://www.parc.com/util/contact.html)." PARC. Retrieved on November 11, 2010. "PARC (Palo Alto Research Center) 3333 Coyote Hill Road Palo Alto, CA 94304 USA"

[3] " driving & public transportation directions (http://www.parc.com/util/directions.html)." PARC. Retrieved on November 11, 2010.

[4] " map (http://www.parc.com/util/map.html)." PARC. Retrieved on November 11, 2010.

[5] Map of Stanford Research Park (http://lbre.stanford.edu/realestate/map) on Stanford University Real Estate web site

[6] Xerox PARC was the first research group to widely adopt the mouse invented by Douglas Engelbart's Augmentation Research Center at the Stanford Research Institute (now SRI International) in Menlo Park, California,

[7] Gladwell, Malcolm (2011-05-11). "Creation Myth: Xerox PARC, Apple, and the truth about innovation" (http://www.newyorker.com/reporting/2011/05/16/110516fa_fact_gladwell). The New Yorker. . Retrieved 2011-10-09.

[8] Pollack, Andrew (1990-03-24). "Most of Xerox's Suit Against Apple Barred" (http://query.nytimes.com/gst/fullpage.html?res=9C0CE3D91E38F937A15750C0A966958260). The New York Times. . Retrieved 2008-12-01.

[9] "Milestones, PARC, a Xerox company" (http://www.parc.com/about/milestones.html). .

Further reading

- Michael A. Hiltzik, *Dealers of Lightning: Xerox PARC and the Dawn of the Computer Age* (HarperCollins, New York, 1999) ISBN 0-88730-989-5
- Douglas K. Smith, Robert C. Alexander, *Fumbling the Future: How Xerox Invented, Then Ignored, the First Personal Computer* (William Morrow and Company, New York, 1988) ISBN 1-58348-266-0
- M. Mitchell Waldrop, *The Dream Machine: J.C.R. Licklider and the Revolution That Made Computing Personal* (Viking Penguin, New York, 2001) ISBN 0-670-89976-3
- Howard Rheingold, *Tools for Thought* (MIT Press, 2000) ISBN 0-262-68115-3

External links

- PARC official web site (http://www.parc.com/)
- Xerox PARC innovation (http://www.xerox.com/innovation/parc.shtml)
- Xerox Star Historical Documents (http://www.digibarn.com/friends/curbow/star/index.html)
- MacKiDo article (http://www.mackido.com/Interface/ui_history.html)

- Oral history interview with Terry Allen Winograd (http://purl.umn.edu/107717) Charles Babbage Institute, University of Minnesota, Minneapolis
- Oral history interview with Paul A. Strassmann (http://purl.umn.edu/107640) Charles Babbage Institute, University of Minnesota, Minneapolis
- Oral history interview with William Crowther (http://purl.umn.edu/107349) Charles Babbage Institute, University of Minnesota, Minneapolis

Strategic_Computing_Initiative

The United States government's **Strategic Computing Initiative** funded research into advanced computer hardware and artificial intelligence from 1983 to 1993. The initiative was designed to support various projects that were required to develop machine intelligence in a prescribed ten-year time frame, from chip design and manufacture, computer architecture to artificial intelligence software. The Department of Defense spent a total of $1 billion on the project.[1]

The inspiration for the program was Japan's fifth generation computer project, an enormous initiative that set aside billions for research into computing and artificial intelligence. As with Sputnik in 1959, the American government saw the Japanese project as a challenge to its technological dominance.[2] The British government also funded a program of their own around the same time, known as Alvey, and a consortium of U.S. companies funded another similar project, the Microelectronics and Computer Technology Corporation.[3] [4]

The goal of SCI, and other contemporary projects, was nothing less than full machine intelligence. "The machine envisioned by SC", according to Alex Roland and Philip Shiman, "would run ten billion instructions per second to see, hear, speak, and think like a human. The degree of integration required would rival that achieved by the human brain, the most complex instrument known to man."[5]

The initiative was conceived as an integrated program, similar to the Apollo moon program,[5] where different subsystems would be created by various companies and academic projects and eventually brought together into a single integrated system. Roland and Shiman wrote that "While most research programs entail tactics or strategy, SC boasted grand strategy, a master plan for an entire campaign."[1]

The project was funded by the Defense Advanced Research Projects Agency and directed by the Information Processing Technology Office (IPTO). By 1985 it had spent $100 million, and 92 projects were underway at 60 institutions: half in industry, half in universities and government labs.[2] Robert Kahn, who directed IPTO in those years, provided the project with its early leadership and inspiration.[6]

By the late 1980s, it became apparent that the project would not succeed in creating machine intelligence at the levels that had been hoped for. Insiders in the program cited problems in communication, organization, and integration.[7] When Jack Schwarz ascended to the leadership of IPTO in 1987, he cut funding to artificial intelligence research (the software component) "deeply and brutally", "eviscerating" the program (wrote Pamela McCorduck).[7] Schwarz felt that DARPA should focus its funding only on those technologies which showed the most promise. In his words, DARPA should "surf", rather than "dog paddle", and he felt strongly AI was not "the next wave".[7]

Although the program failed to meet its goal of high-level machine intelligence,[1] it did help to advance the state of the art of computer hardware to a considerable degree. On the software side, the initiative funded development of the Dynamic Analysis and Replanning Tool, a program that handled logistics using artificial intelligence techniques. This was a huge success, saving the Department of Defense billions during Desert Storm.[4]

The project was superseded in the 1990s by the Accelerated Strategic Computing Initiative and then by the Advanced Simulation and Computing Program. These later programs did not include artificial general intelligence as a goal, but instead focused on supercomputing for large scale simulation, such as atomic bomb simulations.

See also

- Cutbacks at the Strategic Computing Initiative (in AI winter)
- Advanced Simulation and Computing Program

Notes

[1] Roland & Shiman 2002, p. 2
[2] McCorduck 2004, pp. 426–429
[3] Crevier 1993, p. 240
[4] Russell & Norvig 2003, p. 25
[5] Roland & Shiman 2002, p. 4
[6] Roland & Shiman 2002, p. 7
[7] McCorduck 2004, pp. 430–431

References

- Crevier, Daniel (1993), *AI: The Tumultuous Search for Artificial Intelligence*, New York, NY: BasicBooks, ISBN 0-465-02997-3
- McCorduck, Pamela (2004), *Machines Who Think* (http://www.pamelamc.com/html/machines_who_think. html) (2nd ed.), Natick, MA: A. K. Peters, Ltd., ISBN 1-56881-205-1, pp. 426–432
- Roland, Alex; Shiman, Philip (2002). *Strategic Computing: DARPA and the Quest for Machine Intelligence, 1983-1993*. Cambridge, Mass.: MIT Press. ISBN 0-262-18226-2.
- Russell, Stuart J.; Norvig, Peter (2003), *Artificial Intelligence: A Modern Approach* (http://aima.cs.berkeley. edu/) (2nd ed.), Upper Saddle River, New Jersey: Prentice Hall, ISBN 0-13-790395-2

Artificial_intelligence

Artificial intelligence (**AI**) is the intelligence of machines and the branch of computer science that aims to create it. AI textbooks define the field as "the study and design of intelligent agents"[1] where an intelligent agent is a system that perceives its environment and takes actions that maximize its chances of success.[2] John McCarthy, who coined the term in 1956,[3] defines it as "the science and engineering of making intelligent machines."[4]

AI research is highly technical and specialized, deeply divided into subfields that often fail to communicate with each other.[5] Some of the division is due to social and cultural factors: subfields have grown up around particular institutions and the work of individual researchers. AI research is also divided by several technical issues. There are subfields which are focussed on the solution of specific problems, on one of several possible approaches, on the use of widely differing tools and towards the accomplishment of particular applications. The central problems of AI include such traits as reasoning, knowledge, planning, learning, communication, perception and the ability to move and manipulate objects.[6] General intelligence (or "strong AI") is still among the field's long term goals.[7] Currently popular approaches include statistical methods, computational intelligence and traditional symbolic AI. There are enormous number of tools used in AI, including versions of search and mathematical optimization, logic, methods based on probability and economics, and many others.

The field was founded on the claim that a central property of humans, intelligence—the sapience of *Homo sapiens*—can be so precisely described that it can be simulated by a machine.[8] This raises philosophical issues about the nature of the mind and the ethics of creating artificial beings, issues which have been addressed by myth, fiction and philosophy since antiquity.[9] Artificial intelligence has been the subject of optimism,[10] but has also suffered setbacks[11] and, today, has become an essential part of the technology industry, providing the heavy lifting for many of the most difficult problems in computer science.[12]

History

Thinking machines and artificial beings appear in Greek myths, such as Talos of Crete, the bronze robot of Hephaestus, and Pygmalion's Galatea.[13] Human likenesses believed to have intelligence were built in every major civilization: animated cult images were worshipped in Egypt and Greece[14] and humanoid automatons were built by Yan Shi, Hero of Alexandria and Al-Jazari.[15] It was also widely believed that artificial beings had been created by Jābir ibn Hayyān, Judah Loew and Paracelsus.[16] By the 19th and 20th centuries, artificial beings had become a common feature in fiction, as in Mary Shelley's *Frankenstein* or Karel Čapek's *R.U.R. (Rossum's Universal Robots)*.[17] Pamela McCorduck argues that all of these are examples of an ancient urge, as she describes it, "to forge the gods".[9] Stories of these creatures and their fates discuss many of the same hopes, fears and ethical concerns that are presented by artificial intelligence.

Mechanical or "formal" reasoning has been developed by philosophers and mathematicians since antiquity. The study of logic led directly to the invention of the programmable digital electronic computer, based on the work of mathematician Alan Turing and others. Turing's theory of computation suggested that a machine, by shuffling symbols as simple as "0" and "1", could simulate any conceivable(Imaginable) act of mathematical deduction.[18] [19] This, along with concurrent discoveries in neurology, information theory and cybernetics, inspired a small group of researchers to begin to seriously consider the possibility of building an electronic brain.[20]

The field of AI research was founded at a conference on the campus of Dartmouth College in the summer of 1956.[21] The attendees, including John McCarthy, Marvin Minsky, Allen Newell and Herbert Simon, became the leaders of AI research for many decades.[22] They and their students wrote programs that were, to most people, simply astonishing:[23] Computers were solving word problems in algebra, proving logical theorems and speaking English.[24] By the middle of the 1960s, research in the U.S. was heavily funded by the Department of Defense[25] and laboratories had been established around the world.[26] AI's founders were profoundly optimistic about the future of the new field: Herbert Simon predicted that "machines will be capable, within twenty years, of doing any work a man can do" and Marvin Minsky agreed, writing that "within a generation ... the problem of creating 'artificial intelligence' will substantially be solved".[27]

They had failed to recognize the difficulty of some of the problems they faced.[28] In 1974, in response to the criticism of Sir James Lighthill and ongoing pressure from the US Congress to fund more productive projects, both the U.S. and British governments cut off all undirected exploratory research in AI. The next few years, when funding for projects was hard to find, would later be called the "AI winter".[29]

In the early 1980s, AI research was revived by the commercial success of expert systems,[30] a form of AI program that simulated the knowledge and analytical skills of one or more human experts. By 1985 the market for AI had reached over a billion dollars. At the same time, Japan's fifth generation computer project inspired the U.S and British governments to restore funding for academic research in the field.[31] However, beginning with the collapse of the Lisp Machine market in 1987, AI once again fell into disrepute, and a second, longer lasting AI winter began.[32]

In the 1990s and early 21st century, AI achieved its greatest successes, albeit somewhat behind the scenes. Artificial intelligence is used for logistics, data mining, medical diagnosis and many other areas throughout the technology industry.[12] The success was due to several factors: the increasing computational power of computers (see Moore's law), a greater emphasis on solving specific subproblems, the creation of new ties between AI and other fields working on similar problems, and a new commitment by researchers to solid mathematical methods and rigorous scientific standards.[33]

On 11 May 1997, Deep Blue became the first computer chess-playing system to beat a reigning world chess champion, Garry Kasparov.[34] In 2005, a Stanford robot won the DARPA Grand Challenge by driving autonomously for 131 miles along an unrehearsed desert trail.[35] Two years later, a team from CMU won the DARPA Urban Challenge when their vehicle autonomously navigated 55 miles in an Urban environment while adhering to traffic hazards and all traffic laws.[36] In February 2011, in a Jeopardy! quiz show exhibition match, IBM's question answering system, Watson, defeated the two greatest Jeopardy! champions, Brad Rutter and Ken Jennings, by a significant margin.[37]

The leading-edge definition of artificial intelligence research is changing over time. One pragmatic definition is: "AI research is that which computing scientists do not know how to do cost-effectively today." For example, in 1956 optical character recognition (OCR) was considered AI, but today, sophisticated OCR software with a context-sensitive spell checker and grammar checker software comes for free with most image scanners. No one would any longer consider already-solved computing science problems like OCR "artificial intelligence" today.

Low-cost entertaining chess-playing software is commonly available for tablet computers. DARPA no longer provides significant funding for chess-playing computing system development. The Kinect which provides a 3D body−motion interface for the Xbox 360 uses algorithms that emerged from lengthy AI research,[38] but few consumers realize the technology source.

AI applications are no longer the exclusive domain of U.S. Department of Defense R&D, but are now commonplace consumer items and inexpensive intelligent toys.

In common usage, the term "AI" no longer seems to apply to off-the-shelf solved computing-science problems, which may have originally emerged out of years of AI research.

Problems

The general problem of simulating (or creating) intelligence has been broken down into a number of specific sub-problems. These consist of particular traits or capabilities that researchers would like an intelligent system to display. The traits described below have received the most attention.[6]

Deduction, reasoning, problem solving

Early AI researchers developed algorithms that imitated the step-by-step reasoning that humans use when they solve puzzles or make logical deductions.[39] By the late 1980s and '90s, AI research had also developed highly successful methods for dealing with uncertain or incomplete information, employing concepts from probability and economics.[40]

For difficult problems, most of these algorithms can require enormous computational resources – most experience a "combinatorial explosion": the amount of memory or computer time required becomes astronomical when the problem goes beyond a certain size. The search for more efficient problem-solving algorithms is a high priority for AI research.[41]

Human beings solve most of their problems using fast, intuitive judgments rather than the conscious, step-by-step deduction that early AI research was able to model.[42] AI has made some progress at imitating this kind of "sub-symbolic" problem solving: embodied agent approaches emphasize the importance of sensorimotor skills to higher reasoning; neural net research attempts to simulate the structures inside human and animal brains that give rise to this skill; statistical approaches to AI mimic the probabilistic nature of the human ability to guess.

Knowledge representation

Knowledge representation[43] and knowledge engineering[44] are central to AI research. Many of the problems machines are expected to solve will require extensive knowledge about the world. Among the things that AI needs to represent are: objects, properties, categories and relations between objects;[45] situations, events, states and time;[46] causes and effects;[47] knowledge about knowledge (what we know about what other people know);[48] and many other, less well researched domains. A representation of "what exists" is an ontology (borrowing a word from traditional philosophy), of which the most general are called upper ontologies.[49]

Among the most difficult problems in knowledge representation are:

Default reasoning and the qualification problem

> Many of the things people know take the form of "working assumptions." For example, if a bird comes up in conversation, people typically picture an animal that is fist sized, sings, and flies. None of these things are true about all birds. John McCarthy identified this problem in 1969[50] as the qualification problem: for any commonsense rule that AI researchers care to represent, there tend to be a huge number of exceptions. Almost nothing is simply true or false in the way that abstract logic requires. AI research has explored a number of solutions to this problem.[51]

The breadth of commonsense knowledge

> The number of atomic facts that the average person knows is astronomical. Research projects that attempt to build a complete knowledge base of commonsense knowledge (e.g., Cyc) require enormous amounts of laborious ontological engineering — they must be built, by hand, one complicated concept at a time.[52] A

An ontology represents knowledge as a set of concepts within a domain and the relationships between those concepts.

major goal is to have the computer understand enough concepts to be able to learn by reading from sources like the internet, and thus be able to add to its own ontology.

The subsymbolic form of some commonsense knowledge

Much of what people know is not represented as "facts" or "statements" that they could express verbally. For example, a chess master will avoid a particular chess position because it "feels too exposed"[53] or an art critic can take one look at a statue and instantly realize that it is a fake.[54] These are intuitions or tendencies that are represented in the brain non-consciously and sub-symbolically.[55] Knowledge like this informs, supports and provides a context for symbolic, conscious knowledge. As with the related problem of sub-symbolic reasoning, it is hoped that situated AI, computational intelligence, or statistical AI will provide ways to represent this kind of knowledge.[55]

Planning

Intelligent agents must be able to set goals and achieve them.[56] They need a way to visualize the future (they must have a representation of the state of the world and be able to make predictions about how their actions will change it) and be able to make choices that maximize the utility (or "value") of the available choices.[57]

In classical planning problems, the agent can assume that it is the only thing acting on the world and it can be certain what the consequences of its actions may be.[58] However, if the agent is not the only actor, it must periodically ascertain whether the world matches its predictions and it must change its plan as this becomes necessary, requiring the agent to reason under uncertainty.[59]

Multi-agent planning uses the cooperation and competition of many agents to achieve a given goal. Emergent behavior such as this is used by evolutionary algorithms and swarm intelligence.[60]

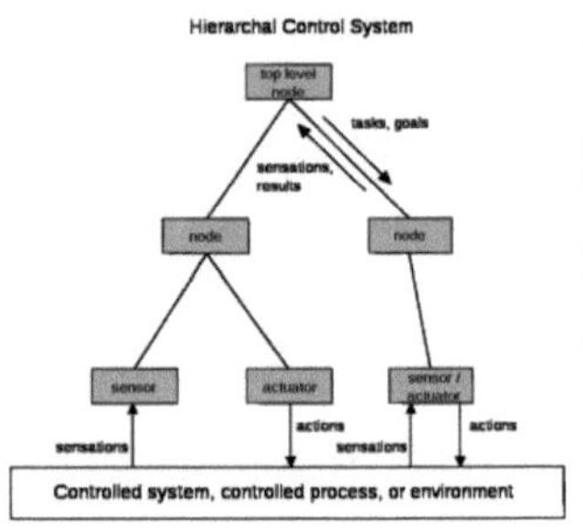

A hierarchical control system is a form of control system in which a set of devices and governing software is arranged in a hierarchy.

Learning

Machine learning[61] has been central to AI research from the beginning.[62] In 1956, at the original Dartmouth AI summer conference, Ray Solomonoff wrote a report on unsupervised probabilistic machine learning: "An Inductive Inference Machine".[63] Unsupervised learning is the ability to find patterns in a stream of input. Supervised learning includes both classification and numerical regression. Classification is used to determine what category something belongs in, after seeing a number of examples of things from several categories. Regression is the attempt to produce a function that describes the relationship between inputs and outputs and predicts how the outputs should change as the inputs change. In reinforcement learning[64] the agent is rewarded for good responses and punished for bad ones. These can be analyzed in terms of decision theory, using concepts like utility. The mathematical analysis of machine learning algorithms and their performance is a branch of theoretical computer science known as computational learning theory.[65]

Natural language processing

Natural language processing[66] gives machines the ability to read and understand the languages that humans speak. A sufficiently powerful natural language processing system would enable natural language user interfaces and the acquisition of knowledge directly from human-written sources, such as Internet texts. Some straightforward applications of natural language processing include information retrieval (or text mining) and machine translation.[67]

A common method of processing and extracting meaning from natural language is through semantic indexing. Increases in processing speeds and the drop in the cost of data storage makes indexing large volumes of abstractions of the users input much more efficient.

A parse tree represents the syntactic structure of a sentence according to some formal grammar.

Motion and manipulation

The field of robotics[68] is closely related to AI. Intelligence is required for robots to be able to handle such tasks as object manipulation[69] and navigation, with sub-problems of localization (knowing where you are), mapping (learning what is around you) and motion planning (figuring out how to get there).[70]

Perception

Machine perception[71] is the ability to use input from sensors (such as cameras, microphones, sonar and others more exotic) to deduce aspects of the world. Computer vision[72] is the ability to analyze visual input. A few selected subproblems are speech recognition,[73] facial recognition and object recognition.[74]

Social intelligence

Affective computing is the study and development of systems and devices that can recognize, interpret, process, and simulate human affects.[76] [77] It is an interdisciplinary field spanning computer sciences, psychology, and cognitive science.[78] While the origins of the field may be traced as far back as to early philosophical enquiries into emotion,[79] the more modern branch of computer science originated with Rosalind Picard's 1995 paper[80] on affective computing.[81] [82] A motivation for the research is the ability to simulate empathy. The machine should interpret the emotional state of humans and adapt its behaviour to them, giving an appropriate response for those emotions.

Kismet, a robot with rudimentary social skills[75]

Emotion and social skills[83] play two roles for an intelligent agent. First, it must be able to predict the actions of others, by understanding their motives and emotional states. (This involves elements of game theory, decision theory, as well as the ability to model human emotions and the perceptual skills to detect emotions.) Also, in an effort to facilitate human-computer interaction, an intelligent machine might want to be able to *display* emotions——even if it does not actually experience them itself——in order to appear sensitive to the emotional dynamics of human interaction.

Creativity

A sub-field of AI addresses creativity both theoretically (from a philosophical and psychological perspective) and practically (via specific implementations of systems that generate outputs that can be considered creative, or systems that identify and assess creativity). Related areas of computational research are Artificial intuition and Artificial imagination.

General intelligence

Most researchers hope that their work will eventually be incorporated into a machine with *general* intelligence (known as strong AI), combining all the skills above and exceeding human abilities at most or all of them.[7] A few believe that anthropomorphic features like artificial consciousness or an artificial brain may be required for such a project.[84] [85]

Many of the problems above are considered AI-complete: to solve one problem, you must solve them all. For example, even a straightforward, specific task like machine translation requires that the machine follow the author's argument (reason), know what is being talked about (knowledge), and faithfully reproduce the author's intention (social intelligence). Machine translation, therefore, is believed to be AI-complete: it may require strong AI to be done as well as humans can do it.[86]

Approaches

There is no established unifying theory or paradigm that guides AI research. Researchers disagree about many issues.[87] A few of the most long standing questions that have remained unanswered are these: should artificial intelligence simulate natural intelligence by studying psychology or neurology? Or is human biology as irrelevant to AI research as bird biology is to aeronautical engineering?[88] Can intelligent behavior be described using simple, elegant principles (such as logic or optimization)? Or does it necessarily require solving a large number of completely unrelated problems?[89] Can intelligence be reproduced using high-level symbols, similar to words and ideas? Or does it require "sub-symbolic" processing?[90] John Haugeland, who coined the term GOFAI (Good Old-Fashioned Artificial Intelligence), also proposed that AI should more properly be referred to as synthetic intelligence,[91] a term which has since been adopted by some non-GOFAI researchers.[92] [93]

Cybernetics and brain simulation

In the 1940s and 1950s, a number of researchers explored the connection between neurology, information theory, and cybernetics. Some of them built machines that used electronic networks to exhibit rudimentary intelligence, such as W. Grey Walter's turtles and the Johns Hopkins Beast. Many of these researchers gathered for meetings of the Teleological Society at Princeton University and the Ratio Club in England.[20] By 1960, this approach was largely abandoned, although elements of it would be revived in the 1980s.

Symbolic

When access to digital computers became possible in the middle 1950s, AI research began to explore the possibility that human intelligence could be reduced to symbol manipulation. The research was centered in three institutions: CMU, Stanford and MIT, and each one developed its own style of research. John Haugeland named these approaches to AI "good old fashioned AI" or "GOFAI".[94] During the 1960s, symbolic approaches had achieved great success at simulating high-level thinking in small demonstration programs. Approaches based on cybernetics or neural networks were abandoned or pushed into the background.[95] Researchers in the 1960s and the 1970s were convinced that symbolic approaches would eventually succeed in creating a machine with artificial general intelligence and considered this the goal of their field.

Cognitive simulation

Economist Herbert Simon and Allen Newell studied human problem-solving skills and attempted to formalize them, and their work laid the foundations of the field of artificial intelligence, as well as cognitive science, operations research and management science. Their research team used the results of psychological experiments to develop programs that simulated the techniques that people used to solve problems. This tradition, centered at Carnegie Mellon University would eventually culminate in the development of the Soar architecture in the middle 80s.[96] [97]

Logic-based

Unlike Newell and Simon, John McCarthy felt that machines did not need to simulate human thought, but should instead try to find the essence of abstract reasoning and problem solving, regardless of whether people used the same algorithms.[88] His laboratory at Stanford (SAIL) focused on using formal logic to solve a wide variety of problems, including knowledge representation, planning and learning.[98] Logic was also focus of the work at the University of Edinburgh and elsewhere in Europe which led to the development of the programming language Prolog and the science of logic programming.[99]

"Anti-logic" or "scruffy"

Researchers at MIT (such as Marvin Minsky and Seymour Papert)[100] found that solving difficult problems in vision and natural language processing required ad-hoc solutions – they argued that there was no simple and general principle (like logic) that would capture all the aspects of intelligent behavior. Roger Schank described their "anti-logic" approaches as "scruffy" (as opposed to the "neat" paradigms at CMU and Stanford).[89] Commonsense knowledge bases (such as Doug Lenat's Cyc) are an example of "scruffy" AI, since they must be built by hand, one complicated concept at a time.[101]

Knowledge-based

When computers with large memories became available around 1970, researchers from all three traditions began to build knowledge into AI applications.[102] This "knowledge revolution" led to the development and deployment of expert systems (introduced by Edward Feigenbaum), the first truly successful form of AI software.[30] The knowledge revolution was also driven by the realization that enormous amounts of knowledge would be required by many simple AI applications.

Sub-symbolic

By the 1980s progress in symbolic AI seemed to stall and many believed that symbolic systems would never be able to imitate all the processes of human cognition, especially perception, robotics, learning and pattern recognition. A number of researchers began to look into "sub-symbolic" approaches to specific AI problems.[90]

Bottom-up, embodied, situated, behavior-based or nouvelle AI

Researchers from the related field of robotics, such as Rodney Brooks, rejected symbolic AI and focused on the basic engineering problems that would allow robots to move and survive.[103] Their work revived the non-symbolic viewpoint of the early cybernetics researchers of the 50s and reintroduced the use of control theory in AI. This coincided with the development of the embodied mind thesis in the related field of cognitive science: the idea that aspects of the body (such as movement, perception and visualization) are required for higher intelligence.

Computational Intelligence

Interest in neural networks and "connectionism" was revived by David Rumelhart and others in the middle 1980s.[104] These and other sub-symbolic approaches, such as fuzzy systems and evolutionary computation, are now studied collectively by the emerging discipline of computational intelligence.[105]

Statistical

In the 1990s, AI researchers developed sophisticated mathematical tools to solve specific subproblems. These tools are truly scientific, in the sense that their results are both measurable and verifiable, and they have been responsible for many of AI's recent successes. The shared mathematical language has also permitted a high level of collaboration with more established fields (like mathematics, economics or operations research). Stuart Russell and Peter Norvig describe this movement as nothing less than a "revolution" and "the victory of the neats."[33] Critiques argue that these techniques are too focussed on particular problems and have failed to address the long term goal of general intelligence.[106]

Integrating the approaches

Intelligent agent paradigm

> An intelligent agent is a system that perceives its environment and takes actions which maximize its chances of success. The simplest intelligent agents are programs that solve specific problems. More complicated agents include human beings and organizations of human beings (such as firms). The paradigm gives researchers license to study isolated problems and find solutions that are both verifiable and useful, without agreeing on one single approach. An agent that solves a specific problem can use any approach that works – some agents are symbolic and logical, some are sub-symbolic neural networks and others may use new approaches. The paradigm also gives researchers a common language to communicate with other fields—such as decision theory and economics—that also use concepts of abstract agents. The intelligent agent paradigm became widely accepted during the 1990s.[2]

Agent architectures and cognitive architectures

> Researchers have designed systems to build intelligent systems out of interacting intelligent agents in a multi-agent system.[107] A system with both symbolic and sub-symbolic components is a hybrid intelligent system, and the study of such systems is artificial intelligence systems integration. A hierarchical control system provides a bridge between sub-symbolic AI at its lowest, reactive levels and traditional symbolic AI at its highest levels, where relaxed time constraints permit planning and world modelling.[108] Rodney Brooks' subsumption architecture was an early proposal for such a hierarchical system.[109]

Tools

In the course of 50 years of research, AI has developed a large number of tools to solve the most difficult problems in computer science. A few of the most general of these methods are discussed below.

Search and optimization

Many problems in AI can be solved in theory by intelligently searching through many possible solutions:[110] Reasoning can be reduced to performing a search. For example, logical proof can be viewed as searching for a path that leads from premises to conclusions, where each step is the application of an inference rule.[111] Planning algorithms search through trees of goals and subgoals, attempting to find a path to a target goal, a process called means-ends analysis.[112] Robotics algorithms for moving limbs and grasping objects use local searches in configuration space.[69] Many learning algorithms use search algorithms based on optimization.

Simple exhaustive searches[113] are rarely sufficient for most real world problems: the search space (the number of places to search) quickly grows to astronomical numbers. The result is a search that is too slow or never completes. The solution, for many problems, is to use "heuristics" or "rules of thumb" that eliminate choices that are unlikely to lead to the goal (called "pruning the search tree"). Heuristics supply the program with a "best guess" for the path on which the solution lies.[114]

A very different kind of search came to prominence in the 1990s, based on the mathematical theory of optimization. For many problems, it is possible to begin the search with some form of a guess and then refine the guess incrementally until no more refinements can be made. These algorithms can be visualized as blind hill climbing: we begin the search at a random point on the landscape, and then, by jumps or steps, we keep moving our guess uphill, until we reach the top. Other optimization algorithms are simulated annealing, beam search and random optimization.[115]

Evolutionary computation uses a form of optimization search. For example, they may begin with a population of organisms (the guesses) and then allow them to mutate and recombine, selecting only the fittest to survive each generation (refining the guesses). Forms of evolutionary computation include swarm intelligence algorithms (such as ant colony or particle swarm optimization)[116] and evolutionary algorithms (such as genetic algorithms and genetic programming).[117]

Logic

Logic[118] is used for knowledge representation and problem solving, but it can be applied to other problems as well. For example, the satplan algorithm uses logic for planning[119] and inductive logic programming is a method for learning.[120]

Several different forms of logic are used in AI research. Propositional or sentential logic[121] is the logic of statements which can be true or false. First-order logic[122] also allows the use of quantifiers and predicates, and can express facts about objects, their properties, and their relations with each other. Fuzzy logic,[123] is a version of first-order logic which allows the truth of a statement to be represented as a value between 0 and 1, rather than simply True (1) or False (0). Fuzzy systems can be used for uncertain reasoning and have been widely used in modern industrial and consumer product control systems. Subjective logic[124] models uncertainty in a different and more explicit manner than fuzzy-logic: a given binomial opinion satisfies belief + disbelief + uncertainty = 1 within a Beta distribution. By this method, ignorance can be distinguished from probabilistic statements that an agent makes with high confidence.

Default logics, non-monotonic logics and circumscription[51] are forms of logic designed to help with default reasoning and the qualification problem. Several extensions of logic have been designed to handle specific domains of knowledge, such as: description logics;[45] situation calculus, event calculus and fluent calculus (for representing events and time);[46] causal calculus;[47] belief calculus; and modal logics.[48]

Probabilistic methods for uncertain reasoning

Many problems in AI (in reasoning, planning, learning, perception and robotics) require the agent to operate with incomplete or uncertain information. AI researchers have devised a number of powerful tools to solve these problems using methods from probability theory and economics.[125]

Bayesian networks[126] are a very general tool that can be used for a large number of problems: reasoning (using the Bayesian inference algorithm),[127] learning (using the expectation-maximization algorithm),[128] planning (using decision networks)[129] and perception (using dynamic Bayesian networks).[130] Probabilistic algorithms can also be used for filtering, prediction, smoothing and finding explanations for streams of data, helping perception systems to analyze processes that occur over time (e.g., hidden Markov models or Kalman filters).[130]

A key concept from the science of economics is "utility": a measure of how valuable something is to an intelligent agent. Precise mathematical tools have been developed that analyze how an agent can make choices and plan, using decision theory, decision analysis,[131] information value theory.[57] These tools include models such as Markov decision processes,[132] dynamic decision networks,[130] game theory and mechanism design.[133]

Classifiers and statistical learning methods

The simplest AI applications can be divided into two types: classifiers ("if shiny then diamond") and controllers ("if shiny then pick up"). Controllers do however also classify conditions before inferring actions, and therefore classification forms a central part of many AI systems. Classifiers are functions that use pattern matching to determine a closest match. They can be tuned according to examples, making them very attractive for use in AI. These examples are known as observations or patterns. In supervised learning, each pattern belongs to a certain predefined class. A class can be seen as a decision that has to be made. All the observations combined with their class labels are known as a data set. When a new observation is received, that observation is classified based on previous experience.[134]

A classifier can be trained in various ways; there are many statistical and machine learning approaches. The most widely used classifiers are the neural network,[135] kernel methods such as the support vector machine,[136] k-nearest neighbor algorithm,[137] Gaussian mixture model,[138] naive Bayes classifier,[139] and decision tree.[140] The performance of these classifiers have been compared over a wide range of tasks. Classifier performance depends greatly on the characteristics of the data to be classified. There is no single classifier that works best on all given problems; this is also referred to as the "no free lunch" theorem. Determining a suitable classifier for a given problem is still more an art than science.[141]

Neural networks

The study of artificial neural networks[135] began in the decade before the field AI research was founded, in the work of Walter Pitts and Warren McCullough. Other important early researchers were Frank Rosenblatt, who invented the perceptron and Paul Werbos who developed the backpropagation algorithm.[142]

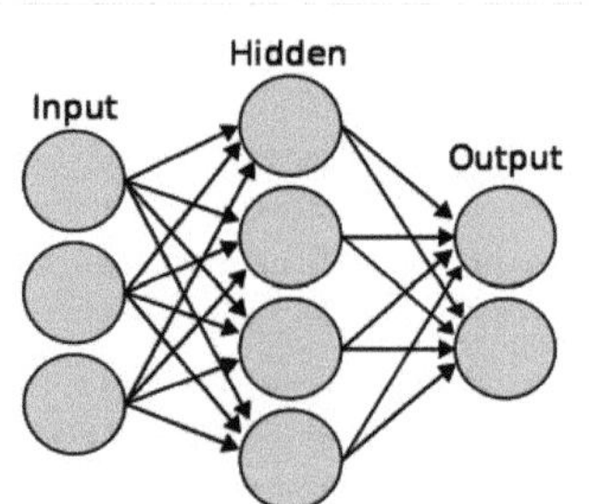

A neural network is an interconnected group of nodes, akin to the vast network of neurons in the human brain.

The main categories of networks are acyclic or feedforward neural networks (where the signal passes in only one direction) and recurrent neural networks (which allow feedback). Among the most popular feedforward networks are perceptrons, multi-layer perceptrons and radial basis networks.[143] Among recurrent networks, the most famous is the Hopfield net, a form of attractor network, which was first described by John Hopfield in 1982.[144] Neural networks can be applied to the problem of intelligent control (for robotics) or learning, using such techniques as Hebbian learning and competitive learning.[145]

Hierarchical temporal memory is an approach that models some of the structural and algorithmic properties of the neocortex.[146]

Control theory

Control theory, the grandchild of cybernetics, has many important applications, especially in robotics.[147]

Languages

AI researchers have developed several specialized languages for AI research, including Lisp[148] and Prolog.[149]

Evaluating progress

In 1950, Alan Turing proposed a general procedure to test the intelligence of an agent now known as the Turing test. This procedure allows almost all the major problems of artificial intelligence to be tested. However, it is a very difficult challenge and at present all agents fail.[150]

Artificial intelligence can also be evaluated on specific problems such as small problems in chemistry, hand-writing recognition and game-playing. Such tests have been termed subject matter expert Turing tests. Smaller problems provide more achievable goals and there are an ever-increasing number of positive results.[151]

The broad classes of outcome for an AI test are: (1) Optimal: it is not possible to perform better. (2) Strong super-human: performs better than all humans. (3) Super-human: performs better than most humans. (4) Sub-human: performs worse than most humans. For example, performance at draughts is optimal,[152] performance at chess is super-human and nearing strong super-human (see Computer chess#Computers versus humans) and performance at many everyday tasks (such as recognizing a face or crossing a room without bumping into something) is sub-human.

A quite different approach measures machine intelligence through tests which are developed from *mathematical* definitions of intelligence. Examples of these kinds of tests start in the late nineties devising intelligence tests using notions from Kolmogorov complexity and data compression.[153] Two major advantages of mathematical definitions are their applicability to nonhuman intelligences and their absence of a requirement for human testers.

Applications

Artificial intelligence techniques are pervasive and are too numerous to list. Frequently, when a technique reaches mainstream use, it is no longer considered artificial intelligence; this phenomenon is described as the AI effect.[154]

Competitions and prizes

There are a number of competitions and prizes to promote research in artificial intelligence. The main areas promoted are: general machine intelligence, conversational behavior, data-mining, driverless cars, robot soccer and games.

Platforms

A platform (or "computing platform") is defined as "some sort of hardware architecture or software framework (including application frameworks), that allows software to run." As Rodney Brooks[155] pointed out many years ago, it is not just the artificial intelligence software that defines the AI features of the platform, but rather the actual platform itself that affects the AI that results, i.e., there needs to be work in AI problems on real-world platforms rather than in isolation.

An automated online assistant providing customer service on a web page – one of many very primitive applications of artificial intelligence.

A wide variety of platforms has allowed different aspects of AI to develop, ranging from expert systems, albeit PC-based but still an entire real-world system, to various robot platforms such as the widely available Roomba with open interface.[156]

Philosophy

Artificial intelligence, by claiming to be able to recreate the capabilities of the human mind, is both a challenge and an inspiration for philosophy. Are there limits to how intelligent machines can be? Is there an essential difference between human intelligence and artificial intelligence? Can a machine have a mind and consciousness? A few of the most influential answers to these questions are given below.[157]

Turing's "polite convention": We need not decide if a machine can "think"; we need only decide if a machine can act as intelligently as a human being. This approach to the philosophical problems associated with artificial intelligence forms the basis of the Turing test.[150]

The Dartmouth proposal: "Every aspect of learning or any other feature of intelligence can be so precisely described that a machine can be made to simulate it." This conjecture was printed in the proposal for the Dartmouth Conference of 1956, and represents the position of most working AI researchers.[158]

Newell and Simon's physical symbol system hypothesis: "A physical symbol system has the necessary and sufficient means of general intelligent action." Newell and Simon argue that intelligences consist of formal operations on symbols.[159] Hubert Dreyfus argued that, on the contrary, human expertise depends on unconscious instinct rather than conscious symbol manipulation and on having a "feel" for the situation rather than explicit symbolic knowledge. (See Dreyfus' critique of AI.)[160] [161]

Gödel's incompleteness theorem: A formal system (such as a computer program) cannot prove all true statements.[162] Roger Penrose is among those who claim that Gödel's theorem limits what machines can do. (See *The Emperor's New Mind*.)[163]

Searle's strong AI hypothesis: "The appropriately programmed computer with the right inputs and outputs would thereby have a mind in exactly the same sense human beings have minds."[164] John Searle counters this assertion with his Chinese room argument, which asks us to look *inside* the computer and try to find where the "mind" might be.[165]

The artificial brain argument: The brain can be simulated. Hans Moravec, Ray Kurzweil and others have argued that it is technologically feasible to copy the brain directly into hardware and software, and that such a simulation will be essentially identical to the original.[85]

Predictions and ethics

Artificial Intelligence is a common topic in both science fiction and projections about the future of technology and society. The existence of an artificial intelligence that rivals human intelligence raises difficult ethical issues, and the potential power of the technology inspires both hopes and fears.

In fiction, Artificial Intelligence has appeared fulfilling many roles, including a servant (R2D2 in *Star Wars*), a law enforcer (K.I.T.T. "Knight Rider"), a comrade (Lt. Commander Data in *Star Trek: The Next Generation*), a conqueror/overlord (*The Matrix*), a dictator (*With Folded Hands*), a benevolent provider/de facto ruler (*The Culture*), an assassin (*Terminator*), a sentient race (*Battlestar Galactica*/Transformers/*Mass Effect*), an extension to human abilities (*Ghost in the Shell*) and the savior of the human race (R. Daneel Olivaw in Isaac Asimov's *Robot* series).

Mary Shelley's *Frankenstein* considers a key issue in the ethics of artificial intelligence: if a machine can be created that has intelligence, could it also *feel*? If it can feel, does it have the same rights as a human? The idea also appears in modern science fiction, including the films *I Robot*, *Blade Runner* and *A.I.: Artificial Intelligence*, in which humanoid machines have the ability to feel human emotions. This issue, now known as "robot rights", is currently being considered by, for example, California's Institute for the Future, although many critics believe that the discussion is premature.[166] The subject is profoundly discussed in the 2010 documentary film *Plug & Pray*.[167]

Martin Ford, author of *The Lights in the Tunnel: Automation, Accelerating Technology and the Economy of the Future*,[168] and others argue that specialized artificial intelligence applications, robotics and other forms of automation will ultimately result in significant unemployment as machines begin to match and exceed the capability of workers to perform most routine and repetitive jobs. Ford predicts that many knowledge-based occupations—and in particular entry level jobs—will be increasingly susceptible to automation via expert systems, machine learning[169] and other AI-enhanced applications. AI-based applications may also be used to amplify the capabilities of low-wage offshore workers, making it more feasible to outsource knowledge work.[170]

Joseph Weizenbaum wrote that AI applications can not, by definition, successfully simulate genuine human empathy and that the use of AI technology in fields such as customer service or psychotherapy[171] was deeply misguided. Weizenbaum was also bothered that AI researchers (and some philosophers) were willing to view the human mind as nothing more than a computer program (a position now known as computationalism). To Weizenbaum these points suggest that AI research devalues human life.[172]

Many futurists believe that artificial intelligence will ultimately transcend the limits of progress. Ray Kurzweil has used Moore's law (which describes the relentless exponential improvement in digital technology) to calculate that desktop computers will have the same processing power as human brains by the year 2029. He also predicts that by 2045 artificial intelligence will reach a point where it is able to improve *itself* at a rate that far exceeds anything conceivable in the past, a scenario that science fiction writer Vernor Vinge named the "singularity".[173]

Robot designer Hans Moravec, cyberneticist Kevin Warwick and inventor Ray Kurzweil have predicted that humans and machines will merge in the future into cyborgs that are more capable and powerful than either.[174] This idea, called transhumanism, which has roots in Aldous Huxley and Robert Ettinger, has been illustrated in fiction as well, for example in the manga *Ghost in the Shell* and the science-fiction series *Dune*.

Edward Fredkin argues that "artificial intelligence is the next stage in evolution", an idea first proposed by Samuel Butler's "Darwin among the Machines" (1863), and expanded upon by George Dyson in his book of the same name in 1998.[175]

Pamela McCorduck writes that all these scenarios are expressions of the ancient human desire to, as she calls it, "forge the gods".[9]

See also

- AI-complete
- Artificial intelligence in fiction
- Artificial Intelligence (journal)
- Artificial intelligence (video games)
- Synthetic intelligence
- Cognitive sciences
- Human Cognome Project
- Friendly artificial intelligence
- List of basic artificial intelligence topics
- List of AI researchers
- List of important AI publications
- List of AI projects
- List of machine learning algorithms
- List of emerging technologies
- List of scientific journals
- Philosophy of mind
- Technological singularity

- Never-Ending Language Learning

References

Notes

[1] Definition of AI as the study of intelligent agents:

- Poole, Mackworth & Goebel 1998, p. 1 (http://people.cs.ubc.ca/~poole/ci/ch1.pdf), which provides the version that is used in this article. Note that they use the term "computational intelligence" as a synonym for artificial intelligence.
- Russell & Norvig (2003) (who prefer the term "rational agent") and write "The whole-agent view is now widely accepted in the field" (Russell & Norvig 2003, p. 55).
- Nilsson 1998

[2] The intelligent agent paradigm:

- Russell & Norvig 2003, pp. 27, 32–58, 968–972
- Poole, Mackworth & Goebel 1998, pp. 7–21
- Luger & Stubblefield 2004, pp. 235–240

The definition used in this article, in terms of goals, actions, perception and environment, is due to Russell & Norvig (2003). Other definitions also include knowledge and learning as additional criteria.

[3] Although there is some controversy on this point (see Crevier (1993, p. 50)), McCarthy states unequivocally "I came up with the term" in a clnet interview. (Skillings 2006)

[4] McCarthy's definition of AI:

- McCarthy 2007

[5] Pamela McCorduck (2004, pp. 424) writes of "the rough shattering of AI in subfields—vision, natural language, decision theory, genetic algorithms, robotics ... and these with own sub-subfield—that would hardly have anything to say to each other."

[6] This list of intelligent traits is based on the topics covered by the major AI textbooks, including:

- Russell & Norvig 2003
- Luger & Stubblefield 2004
- Poole, Mackworth & Goebel 1998
- Nilsson 1998

[7] General intelligence (strong AI) is discussed in popular introductions to AI:

- Kurzweil 1999 and Kurzweil 2005

[8] See the Dartmouth proposal, under Philosophy, below.

[9] This is a central idea of Pamela McCorduck's *Machines That Think*. She writes: "I like to think of artificial intelligence as the scientific apotheosis of a venerable cultural tradition." (McCorduck 2004, p. 34) "Artificial intelligence in one form or another is an idea that has pervaded Western intellectual history, a dream in urgent need of being realized." (McCorduck 2004, p. xviii) "Our history is full of attempts—nutty, eerie, comical, earnest, legendary and real—to make artificial intelligences, to reproduce what is the essential us—bypassing the ordinary means. Back and forth between myth and reality, our imaginations supplying what our workshops couldn't, we have engaged for a long time in this odd form of self-reproduction." (McCorduck 2004, p. 3) She traces the desire back to its Hellenistic roots and calls it the urge to "forge the Gods." (McCorduck 2004, pp. 340–400)

[10] The optimism referred to includes the predictions of early AI researchers (see optimism in the history of AI) as well as the ideas of modern transhumanists such as Ray Kurzweil.

[11] The "setbacks" referred to include the ALPAC report of 1966, the abandonment of perceptrons in 1970, the Lighthill Report of 1973 and the collapse of the lisp machine market in 1987.

[12] AI applications widely used behind the scenes:

- Russell & Norvig 2003, p. 28
- Kurzweil 2005, p. 265
- NRC 1999, pp. 216–222

[13] AI in myth:

- McCorduck 2004, pp. 4–5
- Russell & Norvig 2003, p. 939

[14] Cult images as artificial intelligence:

- Crevier (1993, p. 1) (statue of Amun)
- McCorduck (2004, pp. 6–9)

These were the first machines to be believed to have true intelligence and consciousness. Hermes Trismegistus expressed the common belief that with these statues, craftsman had reproduced "the true nature of the gods", their *sensus* and *spiritus*. McCorduck makes the connection between sacred automatons and Mosaic law (developed around the same time), which expressly forbids the worship of robots (McCorduck

2004, pp. 6–9)

[15] Humanoid automata:

Yan Shi:

* Needham 1986, p. 53

Hero of Alexandria:

* McCorduck 2004, p. 6

Al-Jazari:

* "A Thirteenth Century Programmable Robot" (http://www.shef.ac.uk/marcoms/eview/articles58/robot.html). Shef.ac.uk. . Retrieved 25 April 2009.

Wolfgang von Kempelen:

* McCorduck 2004, p. 17

[16] Artificial beings:

Jābir ibn Hayyān's Takwin:

* O'Connor, Kathleen Malone (1994). *The alchemical creation of life (takwin) and other concepts of Genesis in medieval Islam* (http:// repository.upenn.edu/dissertations/AAI9503804). University of Pennsylvania. . Retrieved 10 January 2007.

Judah Loew's Golem:

* McCorduck 2004, pp. 15–16
* Buchanan 2005, p. 50

Paracelsus' Homunculus:

* McCorduck 2004, pp. 13–14

[17] AI in early science fiction.

* McCorduck 2004, pp. 17–25

[18] This insight, that digital computers can simulate any process of formal reasoning, is known as the Church–Turing thesis.

[19] Formal reasoning:

* Berlinski, David (2000). *The Advent of the Algorithm.* Harcourt Books. ISBN 0-15-601391-6. OCLC 46890682.

[20] AI's immediate precursors:

* McCorduck 2004, pp. 51–107
* Crevier 1993, pp. 27–32
* Russell & Norvig 2003, pp. 15, 940
* Moravec 1988, p. 3

See also Cybernetics and early neural networks (in History of artificial intelligence). Among the researchers who laid the foundations of AI were Alan Turing, John Von Neumann, Norbert Wiener, Claude Shannon, Warren McCullough, Walter Pitts and Donald Hebb.

[21] Dartmouth conference:

* McCorduck 2004, pp. 111–136
* Crevier 1993, pp. 47–49, who writes "the conference is generally recognized as the official birthdate of the new science."
* Russell & Norvig 2003, p. 17, who call the conference "the birth of artificial intelligence."
* NRC 1999, pp. 200–201

[22] Hegemony of the Dartmouth conference attendees:

* Russell & Norvig 2003, p. 17, who write "for the next 20 years the field would be dominated by these people and their students."
* McCorduck 2004, pp. 129–130

[23] Russell and Norvig write "it was astonishing whenever a computer did anything kind of smartish." Russell & Norvig 2003, p. 18

[24] "Golden years" of AI (successful symbolic reasoning programs 1956–1973):

* McCorduck 2004, pp. 243–252
* Crevier 1993, pp. 52–107
* Moravec 1988, p. 9
* Russell & Norvig 2003, pp. 18–21

The programs described are Daniel Bobrow's STUDENT, Newell and Simon's Logic Theorist and Terry Winograd's SHRDLU.

[25] DARPA pours money into undirected pure research into AI during the 1960s:

* McCorduck 2004, pp. 131
* Crevier 1993, pp. 51, 64–65
* NRC 1999, pp. 204–205

[26] AI in England:

* Howe 1994

[27] Optimism of early AI:

* Herbert Simon quote: Simon 1965, p. 96 quoted in Crevier 1993, p. 109.

- Marvin Minsky quote: Minsky 1967, p. 2 quoted in Crevier 1993, p. 109.

[28] See The problems (in History of artificial intelligence)

[29] First AI Winter, Mansfield Amendment, Lighthill report

- Crevier 1993, pp. 115–117
- Russell & Norvig 2003, p. 22
- NRC 1999, pp. 212–213
- Howe 1994

[30] Expert systems:

- ACM 1998, I.2.1,
- Russell & Norvig 2003, pp. 22–24
- Luger & Stubblefield 2004, pp. 227–331,
- Nilsson 1998, chpt. 17.4
- McCorduck 2004, pp. 327–335, 434–435
- Crevier 1993, pp. 145–62, 197–203

[31] Boom of the 1980s: rise of expert systems, Fifth Generation Project, Alvey, MCC, SCI:

- McCorduck 2004, pp. 426–441
- Crevier 1993, pp. 161–162,197–203, 211, 240
- Russell & Norvig 2003, p. 24
- NRC 1999, pp. 210–211

[32] Second AI winter:

- McCorduck 2004, pp. 430–435
- Crevier 1993, pp. 209–210
- NRC 1999, pp. 214–216

[33] Formal methods are now preferred ("Victory of the neats"):

- Russell & Norvig 2003, pp. 25–26
- McCorduck 2004, pp. 486–487

[34] McCorduck 2004, pp. 480–483

[35] DARPA Grand Challenge – home page (http://www.darpa.mil/grandchallenge/)

[36] "Welcome" (http://archive.darpa.mil/grandchallenge/). Archive.darpa.mil. . Retrieved 31 October 2011.

[37] Markoff, John (16 February 2011). "On 'Jeopardy!' Watson Win Is All but Trivial" (http://www.nytimes.com/2011/02/17/science/ 17jeopardy-watson.html). *The New York Times.* .

[38] Kinect's AI breakthrough explained (http://www.i-programmer.info/news/105-artificial-intelligence/ 2176-kinects-ai-breakthrough-explained.html)

[39] Problem solving, puzzle solving, game playing and deduction:

- Russell & Norvig 2003, chpt. 3–9,
- Poole, Mackworth & Goebel 1998, chpt. 2,3,7,9,
- Luger & Stubblefield 2004, chpt. 3,4,6,8,
- Nilsson 1998, chpt. 7–12

[40] Uncertain reasoning:

- Russell & Norvig 2003, pp. 452–644,
- Poole, Mackworth & Goebel 1998, pp. 345–395,
- Luger & Stubblefield 2004, pp. 333–381,
- Nilsson 1998, chpt. 19

[41] Intractability and efficiency and the combinatorial explosion:

- Russell & Norvig 2003, pp. 9, 21–22

[42] Psychological evidence of sub-symbolic reasoning:

- Wason & Shapiro (1966) showed that people do poorly on completely abstract problems, but if the problem is restated to allow the use of intuitive social intelligence, performance dramatically improves. (See Wason selection task)
- Kahneman, Slovic & Tversky (1982) have shown that people are terrible at elementary problems that involve uncertain reasoning. (See list of cognitive biases for several examples).
- Lakoff & Núñez (2000) have controversially argued that even our skills at mathematics depend on knowledge and skills that come from "the body", i.e. sensorimotor and perceptual skills. (See Where Mathematics Comes From)

[43] Knowledge representation:

- ACM 1998, I.2.4,
- Russell & Norvig 2003, pp. 320–363,
- Poole, Mackworth & Goebel 1998, pp. 23–46, 69–81, 169–196, 235–277, 281–298, 319–345,
- Luger & Stubblefield 2004, pp. 227–243,

- Nilsson 1998, chpt. 18

[44] Knowledge engineering:

- Russell & Norvig 2003, pp. 260–266,
- Poole, Mackworth & Goebel 1998, pp. 199–233,
- Nilsson 1998, chpt. ~17.1–17.4

[45] Representing categories and relations: Semantic networks, description logics, inheritance (including frames and scripts):

- Russell & Norvig 2003, pp. 349–354,
- Poole, Mackworth & Goebel 1998, pp. 174–177,
- Luger & Stubblefield 2004, pp. 248–258,
- Nilsson 1998, chpt. 18.3

[46] Representing events and time:Situation calculus, event calculus, fluent calculus (including solving the frame problem):

- Russell & Norvig 2003, pp. 328–341,
- Poole, Mackworth & Goebel 1998, pp. 281–298,
- Nilsson 1998, chpt. 18.2

[47] Causal calculus:

- Poole, Mackworth & Goebel 1998, pp. 335–337

[48] Representing knowledge about knowledge: Belief calculus, modal logics:

- Russell & Norvig 2003, pp. 341–344,
- Poole, Mackworth & Goebel 1998, pp. 275–277

[49] Ontology:

- Russell & Norvig 2003, pp. 320–328

[50] Qualification problem:

- McCarthy & Hayes 1969
- Russell & Norvig 2003

While McCarthy was primarily concerned with issues in the logical representation of actions, Russell & Norvig 2003 apply the term to the more general issue of default reasoning in the vast network of assumptions underlying all our commonsense knowledge.

[51] Default reasoning and default logic, non-monotonic logics, circumscription, closed world assumption, abduction (Poole *et al.* places abduction under "default reasoning". Luger *et al.* places this under "uncertain reasoning"):

- Russell & Norvig 2003, pp. 354–360,
- Poole, Mackworth & Goebel 1998, pp. 248–256, 323–335,
- Luger & Stubblefield 2004, pp. 335–363,
- Nilsson 1998, ~18.3.3

[52] Breadth of commonsense knowledge:

- Russell & Norvig 2003, p. 21,
- Crevier 1993, pp. 113–114,
- Moravec 1988, p. 13,
- Lenat & Guha 1989 (Introduction)

[53] Dreyfus & Dreyfus 1986

[54] Gladwell 2005

[55] Expert knowledge as embodied intuition:

- Dreyfus & Dreyfus 1986 (Hubert Dreyfus is a philosopher and critic of AI who was among the first to argue that most useful human knowledge was encoded sub-symbolically. See Dreyfus' critique of AI)
- Gladwell 2005 (Gladwell's *Blink* is a popular introduction to sub-symbolic reasoning and knowledge.)
- Hawkins & Blakeslee 2005 (Hawkins argues that sub-symbolic knowledge should be the primary focus of AI research.)

[56] Planning:

- ACM 1998, ~I.2.8,
- Russell & Norvig 2003, pp. 375–459,
- Poole, Mackworth & Goebel 1998, pp. 281–316,
- Luger & Stubblefield 2004, pp. 314–329,
- Nilsson 1998, chpt. 10.1–2, 22

[57] Information value theory:

- Russell & Norvig 2003, pp. 600–604

[58] Classical planning:

- Russell & Norvig 2003, pp. 375–430,
- Poole, Mackworth & Goebel 1998, pp. 281–315,
- Luger & Stubblefield 2004, pp. 314–329,

- Nilsson 1998, chpt. 10.1–2, 22

[59] Planning and acting in non-deterministic domains: conditional planning, execution monitoring, replanning and continuous planning:

- Russell & Norvig 2003, pp. 430–449

[60] Multi-agent planning and emergent behavior:

- Russell & Norvig 2003, pp. 449–455

[61] Learning:

- ACM 1998, I.2.6,
- Russell & Norvig 2003, pp. 649–788,
- Poole, Mackworth & Goebel 1998, pp. 397–438,
- Luger & Stubblefield 2004, pp. 385–542,
- Nilsson 1998, chpt. 3.3 , 10.3, 17.5, 20

[62] Alan Turing discussed the centrality of learning as early as 1950, in his classic paper Computing Machinery and Intelligence. (Turing 1950)

[63] (pdf scanned copy of the original) (http://world.std.com/~rjs/indinf56.pdf) (version published in 1957, An Inductive Inference Machine," IRE Convention Record, Section on Information Theory, Part 2, pp. 56–62)

[64] Reinforcement learning:

- Russell & Norvig 2003, pp. 763–788
- Luger & Stubblefield 2004, pp. 442–449

[65] Computational learning theory:

- CITATION IN PROGRESS.

[66] Natural language processing:

- ACM 1998, I.2.7
- Russell & Norvig 2003, pp. 790–831
- Poole, Mackworth & Goebel 1998, pp. 91–104
- Luger & Stubblefield 2004, pp. 591–632

[67] Applications of natural language processing, including information retrieval (i.e. text mining) and machine translation:

- Russell & Norvig 2003, pp. 840–857,
- Luger & Stubblefield 2004, pp. 623–630

[68] Robotics:

- ACM 1998, I.2.9,
- Russell & Norvig 2003, pp. 901–942,
- Poole, Mackworth & Goebel 1998, pp. 443–460

[69] Moving and configuration space:

- Russell & Norvig 2003, pp. 916–932

[70] Robotic mapping (localization, etc):

- Russell & Norvig 2003, pp. 908–915

[71] Machine perception:

- Russell & Norvig 2003, pp. 537–581, 863–898
- Nilsson 1998, ~chpt. 6

[72] Computer vision:

- ACM 1998, I.2.10
- Russell & Norvig 2003, pp. 863–898
- Nilsson 1998, chpt. 6

[73] Speech recognition:

- ACM 1998, ~I.2.7
- Russell & Norvig 2003, pp. 568–578

[74] Object recognition:

- Russell & Norvig 2003, pp. 885–892

[75] "Kismet" (http://www.ai.mit.edu/projects/humanoid-robotics-group/kismet/kismet.html). MIT Artificial Intelligence Laboratory, Humanoid Robotics Group. .

[76] Thro, Ellen (1993). *Robotics*. New York.

[77] Edelson, Edward (1991). *The Nervous System*. New York: Remmel Nunn.

[78] Tao, Jianhua; Tieniu Tan (2005). "Affective Computing: A Review". *Affective Computing and Intelligent Interaction*. **LNCS 3784**. Springer. pp. 981–995. doi:10.1007/11573548.

[79] James, William (1884). "What is Emotion". *Mind* **9**: 188–205. doi:10.1093/mind/os-IX.34.188. Cited by Tao and Tan.

[80] "Affective Computing" (http://affect.media.mit.edu/pdfs/95.picard.pdf) MIT Technical Report #321 (Abstract (http://vismod.media. mit.edu/pub/tech-reports/TR-321-ABSTRACT.html)), 1995

[81] Kleine-Cosack, Christian (October 2006). "Recognition and Simulation of Emotions" (http://web.archive.org/web/20080528135730/
      http://ls12-www.cs.tu-dortmund.de/~fink/lectures/SS06/human-robot-interaction/Emotion-RecognitionAndSimulation.pdf) (PDF).
      Archived from the original (http://ls12-www.cs.tu-dortmund.de//~fink/lectures/SS06/human-robot-interaction/
      Emotion-RecognitionAndSimulation.pdf) on May 28, 2008. . Retrieved May 13, 2008. "The introduction of emotion to computer science was
      done by Pickard (sic) who created the field of affective computing."

[82] Diamond, David (December 2003). "The Love Machine; Building computers that care" (http://www.wired.com/wired/archive/11.12/
      love.html). Wired. . Retrieved May 13, 2008. "Rosalind Picard, a genial MIT professor, is the field's godmother; her 1997 book, Affective
      Computing, triggered an explosion of interest in the emotional side of computers and their users."

[83] Emotion and affective computing:

      • Minsky 2006

[84] Gerald Edelman, Igor Aleksander and others have both argued that artificial consciousness is required for strong AI. (Aleksander 1995;
      Edelman 2007)

[85] Artificial brain arguments: AI requires a simulation of the operation of the human brain

      • Russell & Norvig 2003, p. 957
      • Crevier 1993, pp. 271 and 279

      A few of the people who make some form of the argument:

      • Moravec 1988
      • Kurzweil 2005, p. 262
      • Hawkins & Blakeslee 2005

      The most extreme form of this argument (the brain replacement scenario) was put forward by Clark Glymour in the mid-70s and was touched
      on by Zenon Pylyshyn and John Searle in 1980.

[86] AI complete: Shapiro 1992, p. 9

[87] Nils Nilsson writes: "Simply put, there is wide disagreement in the field about what AI is all about" (Nilsson 1983, p. 10).

[88] Biological intelligence vs. intelligence in general:

      • Russell & Norvig 2003, pp. 2–3, who make the analogy with aeronautical engineering.
      • McCorduck 2004, pp. 100–101, who writes that there are "two major branches of artificial intelligence: one aimed at producing intelligent
         behavior regardless of how it was accomplioshed, and the other aimed at modeling intelligent processes found in nature, particularly
         human ones."
      • Kolata 1982, a paper in *Science*, which describes McCathy's indifference to biological models. Kolata quotes McCarthy as writing: "This
         is AI, so we don't care if it's psychologically real" (http://books.google.com/books?id=PEkqAAAAMAAJ&q="we+don't+care+if+
         it's+psychological+real"&dq="we+don't+care+if+it's+psychological+real"&output=html&pgis=1). McCarthy recently
         reiterated his position at the AI@50 conference where he said "Artificial intelligence is not, by definition, simulation of human
         intelligence" (Maker 2006).

[89] Neats vs. scruffies:

      • McCorduck 2004, pp. 421–424, 486–489
      • Crevier 1993, pp. 168
      • Nilsson 1983, pp. 10–11

[90] Symbolic vs. sub-symbolic AI:

      • Nilsson (1998, p. 7), who uses the term "sub-symbolic".

[91] Haugeland 1985, p. 255

[92] http://citeseerx.ist.psu.edu/viewdoc/download?doi=10.1.1.38.8384&rep=rep1&type=pdf

[93] Pei Wang (2008). *Artificial general intelligence, 2008: proceedings of the First AGI Conference* (http://books.google.com/
      books?id=a_ZR81Z25z0C&pg=PA63). IOS Press. p. 63. ISBN 978-1-58603-833-5. . Retrieved 31 October 2011.

[94] Haugeland 1985, pp. 112–117

[95] The most dramatic case of sub-symbolic AI being pushed into the background was the devastating critique of perceptrons by Marvin Minsky
      and Seymour Papert in 1969. See History of AI, AI winter, or Frank Rosenblatt.

[96] Cognitive simulation, Newell and Simon, AI at CMU (then called Carnegie Tech):

      • McCorduck 2004, pp. 139–179, 245–250, 322–323 (EPAM)
      • Crevier 1993, pp. 145–149

[97] Soar (history):

      • McCorduck 2004, pp. 450–451
      • Crevier 1993, pp. 258–263

[98] McCarthy and AI research at SAIL and SRI International:

      • McCorduck 2004, pp. 251–259
      • Crevier 1993

[99] AI research at Edinburgh and in France, birth of Prolog:

      • Crevier 1993, pp. 193–196

- Howe 1994
[100] AI at MIT under Marvin Minsky in the 1960s :

- McCorduck 2004, pp. 259–305
- Crevier 1993, pp. 83–102, 163–176
- Russell & Norvig 2003, p. 19

[101] Cyc:

- McCorduck 2004, p. 489, who calls it "a determinedly scruffy enterprise"
- Crevier 1993, pp. 239–243
- Russell & Norvig 2003, p. 363–365
- Lenat & Guha 1989

[102] Knowledge revolution:

- McCorduck 2004, pp. 266–276, 298–300, 314, 421
- Russell & Norvig 2003, pp. 22–23

[103] Embodied approaches to AI:

- McCorduck 2004, pp. 454–462
- Brooks 1990
- Moravec 1988

[104] Revival of connectionism:

- Crevier 1993, pp. 214–215
- Russell & Norvig 2003, p. 25

[105] Computational intelligence

- IEEE Computational Intelligence Society (http://www.ieee-cis.org/)

[106] Pat Langley, "The changing science of machine learning" (http://www.springerlink.com/content/j067h855n8223338/), *Machine Learning*, Volume 82, Number 3, 275–279, doi:10.1007/s10994-011-5242-y

[107] Agent architectures, hybrid intelligent systems:

- Russell & Norvig (2003, pp. 27, 932, 970–972)
- Nilsson (1998, chpt. 25)

[108] Hierarchical control system:

- Albus, J. S. 4-D/RCS reference model architecture for unmanned ground vehicles. (http://www.isd.mel.nist.gov/documents/albus/4DRCS.pdf) In G Gerhart, R Gunderson, and C Shoemaker, editors, Proceedings of the SPIE AeroSense Session on Unmanned Ground Vehicle Technology, volume 3693, pages 11—20

[109] Subsumption architecture:

- CITATION IN PROGRESS.

[110] Search algorithms:

- Russell & Norvig 2003, pp. 59–189
- Poole, Mackworth & Goebel 1998, pp. 113–163
- Luger & Stubblefield 2004, pp. 79–164, 193–219
- Nilsson 1998, chpt. 7–12

[111] Forward chaining, backward chaining, Horn clauses, and logical deduction as search:

- Russell & Norvig 2003, pp. 217–225, 280–294
- Poole, Mackworth & Goebel 1998, pp. ~46–52
- Luger & Stubblefield 2004, pp. 62–73
- Nilsson 1998, chpt. 4.2, 7.2

[112] State space search and planning:

- Russell & Norvig 2003, pp. 382–387
- Poole, Mackworth & Goebel 1998, pp. 298–305
- Nilsson 1998, chpt. 10.1–2

[113] Uninformed searches (breadth first search, depth first search and general state space search):

- Russell & Norvig 2003, pp. 59–93
- Poole, Mackworth & Goebel 1998, pp. 113–132
- Luger & Stubblefield 2004, pp. 79–121
- Nilsson 1998, chpt. 8

[114] Heuristic or informed searches (e.g., greedy best first and A*):

- Russell & Norvig 2003, pp. 94–109,
- Poole, Mackworth & Goebel 1998, pp. pp. 132–147,
- Luger & Stubblefield 2004, pp. 133–150,

- Nilsson 1998, chpt. 9
[115] Optimization searches:

- Russell & Norvig 2003, pp. 110–116,120–129
- Poole, Mackworth & Goebel 1998, pp. 56–163
- Luger & Stubblefield 2004, pp. 127–133

[116] Artificial life and society based learning:

- Luger & Stubblefield 2004, pp. 530–541

[117] Genetic programming and genetic algorithms:

- Luger & Stubblefield 2004, pp. 509–530,
- Nilsson 1998, chpt. 4.2.
- Holland, John H. (1975). *Adaptation in Natural and Artificial Systems*. University of Michigan Press. ISBN 0262581116.
- Koza, John R. (1992). *Genetic Programming*. MIT Press. ISBN 0262111705.
- Poli, R., Langdon, W. B., McPhee, N. F. (2008). *A Field Guide to Genetic Programming*. Lulu.com, freely available from http://www. gp-field-guide.org.uk/. ISBN 978-1-4092-0073-4.

[118] Logic:

- ACM 1998, ~I.2.3,
- Russell & Norvig 2003, pp. 194–310,
- Luger & Stubblefield 2004, pp. 35–77,
- Nilsson 1998, chpt. 13–16

[119] Satplan:

- Russell & Norvig 2003, pp. 402–407,
- Poole, Mackworth & Goebel 1998, pp. 300–301,
- Nilsson 1998, chpt. 21

[120] Explanation based learning, relevance based learning, inductive logic programming, case based reasoning:

- Russell & Norvig 2003, pp. 678–710,
- Poole, Mackworth & Goebel 1998, pp. 414–416,
- Luger & Stubblefield 2004, pp. ~422–442,
- Nilsson 1998, chpt. 10.3, 17.5

[121] Propositional logic:

- Russell & Norvig 2003, pp. 204–233,
- Luger & Stubblefield 2004, pp. 45–50
- Nilsson 1998, chpt. 13

[122] First-order logic and features such as equality:

- ACM 1998, ~I.2.4,
- Russell & Norvig 2003, pp. 240–310,
- Poole, Mackworth & Goebel 1998, pp. 268–275,
- Luger & Stubblefield 2004, pp. 50–62,
- Nilsson 1998, chpt. 15

[123] Fuzzy logic:

- Russell & Norvig 2003, pp. 526–527

[124] Subjective logic:

- CITATION IN PROGRESS.

[125] Stochastic methods for uncertain reasoning:

- ACM 1998, ~I.2.3,
- Russell & Norvig 2003, pp. 462–644,
- Poole, Mackworth & Goebel 1998, pp. 345–395,
- Luger & Stubblefield 2004, pp. 165–191, 333–381,
- Nilsson 1998, chpt. 19

[126] Bayesian networks:

- Russell & Norvig 2003, pp. 492–523,
- Poole, Mackworth & Goebel 1998, pp. 361–381,
- Luger & Stubblefield 2004, pp. ~182–190, ~363–379,
- Nilsson 1998, chpt. 19.3–4

[127] Bayesian inference algorithm:

- Russell & Norvig 2003, pp. 504–519,
- Poole, Mackworth & Goebel 1998, pp. 361–381,

- Luger & Stubblefield 2004, pp. ~363–379,
- Nilsson 1998, chpt. 19.4 & 7

[128] Bayesian learning and the expectation-maximization algorithm:

- Russell & Norvig 2003, pp. 712–724,
- Poole, Mackworth & Goebel 1998, pp. 424–433,
- Nilsson 1998, chpt. 20

[129] Bayesian decision theory and Bayesian decision networks:

- Russell & Norvig 2003, pp. 597–600

[130] Stochastic temporal models:

- Russell & Norvig 2003, pp. 537–581

Dynamic Bayesian networks:

- Russell & Norvig 2003, pp. 551–557

Hidden Markov model:

- (Russell & Norvig 2003, pp. 549–551)

Kalman filters:

- Russell & Norvig 2003, pp. 551–557

[131] decision theory and decision analysis:

- Russell & Norvig 2003, pp. 584–597,
- Poole, Mackworth & Goebel 1998, pp. 381–394

[132] Markov decision processes and dynamic decision networks:

- Russell & Norvig 2003, pp. 613–631

[133] Game theory and mechanism design:

- Russell & Norvig 2003, pp. 631–643

[134] Statistical learning methods and classifiers:

- Russell & Norvig 2003, pp. 712–754,
- Luger & Stubblefield 2004, pp. 453–541

[135] Neural networks and connectionism:

- Russell & Norvig 2003, pp. 736–748,
- Poole, Mackworth & Goebel 1998, pp. 408–414,
- Luger & Stubblefield 2004, pp. 453–505,
- Nilsson 1998, chpt. 3

[136] kernel methods such as the support vector machine, Kernel methods:

- Russell & Norvig 2003, pp. 749–752

[137] K-nearest neighbor algorithm:

- Russell & Norvig 2003, pp. 733–736

[138] Gaussian mixture model:

- Russell & Norvig 2003, pp. 725–727

[139] Naive Bayes classifier:

- Russell & Norvig 2003, pp. 718

[140] Decision tree:

- Russell & Norvig 2003, pp. 653–664,
- Poole, Mackworth & Goebel 1998, pp. 403–408,
- Luger & Stubblefield 2004, pp. 408–417

[141] Classifier performance:

- van der Walt & Bernard 2006

[142] Backpropagation:

- Russell & Norvig 2003, pp. 744–748,
- Luger & Stubblefield 2004, pp. 467–474,
- Nilsson 1998, chpt. 3.3

[143] Feedforward neural networks, perceptrons and radial basis networks:

- Russell & Norvig 2003, pp. 739–748, 758
- Luger & Stubblefield 2004, pp. 458–467

[144] Recurrent neural networks, Hopfield nets:

- Russell & Norvig 2003, p. 758

* Luger & Stubblefield 2004, pp. 474–505

[145] Competitive learning, Hebbian coincidence learning, Hopfield networks and attractor networks:

* Luger & Stubblefield 2004, pp. 474–505

[146] Hierarchical temporal memory:

* Hawkins & Blakeslee 2005

[147] Control theory:

* ACM 1998, ~I.2.8,
* Russell & Norvig 2003, pp. 926–932

[148] Lisp:

* Luger & Stubblefield 2004, pp. 723–821
* Crevier 1993, pp. 59–62,
* Russell & Norvig 2003, p. 18

[149] Prolog:

* Poole, Mackworth & Goebel 1998, pp. 477–491,
* Luger & Stubblefield 2004, pp. 641–676, 575–581

[150] The Turing test:

Turing's original publication:

* Turing 1950

Historical influence and philosophical implications:

* Haugeland 1985, pp. 6–9
* Crevier 1993, p. 24
* McCorduck 2004, pp. 70–71
* Russell & Norvig 2003, pp. 2–3 and 948

[151] Subject matter expert Turing test:

* CITATION IN PROGRESS.

[152] Game AI:

* CITATION IN PROGRESS.

[153] Mathematical definitions of intelligence:

* Jose Hernandez-Orallo (2000). "Beyond the Turing Test" (http://citeseerx.ist.psu.edu/viewdoc/summary?doi=10.1.1.44.8943). *Journal of Logic, Language and Information* **9** (4): 447–466. doi:10.1023/A:1008367325700. . Retrieved 21 July 2009.
* D L Dowe and A R Hajek (1997). "A computational extension to the Turing Test" (http://www.csse.monash.edu.au/publications/ 1997/tr-cs97-322-abs.html). *Proceedings of the 4th Conference of the Australasian Cognitive Science jSociety.* . Retrieved 21 July 2009.
* J Hernandez-Orallo and D L Dowe (2010). "Measuring Universal Intelligence: Towards an Anytime Intelligence Test". *Artificial Intelligence Journal* **174** (18): 1508–1539. doi:10.1016/j.artint.2010.09.006.

[154] "AI set to exceed human brain power" (http://www.cnn.com/2006/TECH/science/07/24/ai.bostrom/) (web article). CNN. 26 July 2006. . Retrieved 26 February 2008.

[155] Brooks, R.A., "How to build complete creatures rather than isolated cognitive simulators," in K. VanLehn (ed.), Architectures for Intelligence, pp. 225–239, Lawrence Erlbaum Associates, Hillsdale, NJ, 1991.

[156] Hacking Roomba » Search Results » atmel (http://hackingroomba.com/?s=atmel)

[157] Philosophy of AI. All of these positions in this section are mentioned in standard discussions of the subject, such as:

* Russell & Norvig 2003, pp. 947–960
* Fearn 2007, pp. 38–55

[158] Dartmouth proposal:

* McCarthy et al. 1955 (the original proposal)
* Crevier 1993, p. 49 (historical significance)

[159] The physical symbol systems hypothesis:

* Newell & Simon 1976, p. 116
* McCorduck 2004, p. 153
* Russell & Norvig 2003, p. 18

[160] Dreyfus criticized the necessary condition of the physical symbol system hypothesis, which he called the "psychological assumption": "The mind can be viewed as a device operating on bits of information according to formal rules". (Dreyfus 1992, p. 156)

[161] Dreyfus' critique of artificial intelligence:

* Dreyfus 1972, Dreyfus & Dreyfus 1986
* Crevier 1993, pp. 120–132
* McCorduck 2004, pp. 211–239
* Russell & Norvig 2003, pp. 950–952,

[162] This is a paraphrase of the relevant implication of Gödel's theorems.

[163] The Mathematical Objection:

- Russell & Norvig 2003, p. 949
- McCorduck 2004, pp. 448–449

Making the Mathematical Objection:

- Lucas 1961
- Penrose 1989

Refuting Mathematical Objection:

- Turing 1950 under "(2) The Mathematical Objection"
- Hofstadter 1979

Background:

- Gödel 1931, Church 1936, Kleene 1935, Turing 1937

[164] This version is from Searle (1999), and is also quoted in Dennett 1991, p. 435. Searle's original formulation was "The appropriately programmed computer really is a mind, in the sense that computers given the right programs can be literally said to understand and have other cognitive states." (Searle 1980, p. 1). Strong AI is defined similarly by Russell & Norvig (2003, p. 947): "The assertion that machines could possibly act intelligently (or, perhaps better, act as if they were intelligent) is called the 'weak AI' hypothesis by philosophers, and the assertion that machines that do so are actually thinking (as opposed to simulating thinking) is called the 'strong AI' hypothesis."

[165] Searle's Chinese Room argument:

- Searle 1980. Searle's original presentation of the thought experiment.
- Searle 1999.

Discussion:

- Russell & Norvig 2003, pp. 958–960
- McCorduck 2004, pp. 443–445
- Crevier 1993, pp. 269–271

[166] Robot rights:

- Russell & Norvig 2003, p. 964
- "Robots could demand legal rights" (http://news.bbc.co.uk/2/hi/technology/6200005.stm). *BBC News*. 21 December 2006. . Retrieved 3 February 2011.

Prematurity of:

- Henderson, Mark (24 April 2007). "Human rights for robots? We're getting carried away" (http://www.timesonline.co.uk/tol/news/uk/science/article1695546.ece). *The Times Online* (London). .

In fiction:

- McCorduck (2004, p. 190-25) discusses *Frankenstein* and identifies the key ethical issues as scientific hubris and the suffering of the monster, i.e. robot rights.

[167] Independent documentary Plug & Pray, featuring Joseph Weizenbaum and Raymond Kurzweil (http://www.plugandpray-film.de/en/content.html)

[168] Ford, Martin R. (2009), *The Lights in the Tunnel: Automation, Accelerating Technology and the Economy of the Future* (http://www.thelightsinthetunnel.com), Acculant Publishing, ISBN 978-1448659814, . (*e-book available free online* (http://www.thelightsinthetunnel.com/).)

[169] "Machine Learning: A Job Killer?" (http://econfuture.wordpress.com/2011/04/14/machine-learning-a-job-killer/)

[170] AI could decrease the demand for human labor:

- Russell & Norvig 2003, pp. 960–961
- Ford, Martin (2009). *The Lights in the Tunnel: Automation, Accelerating Technology and the Economy of the Future* (http://www.thelightsinthetunnel.com). Acculant Publishing. ISBN 978-1-4486-5981-4. .

[171] In the early 70s, Kenneth Colby presented a version of Weizenbaum's ELIZA known as DOCTOR which he promoted as a serious therapeutic tool. (Crevier 1993, pp. 132–144)

[172] Joseph Weizenbaum's critique of AI:

- Weizenbaum 1976
- Crevier 1993, pp. 132–144
- McCorduck 2004, pp. 356–373
- Russell & Norvig 2003, p. 961

Weizenbaum (the AI researcher who developed the first chatterbot program, ELIZA) argued in 1976 that the misuse of artificial intelligence has the potential to devalue human life.

[173] Technological singularity:

- Vinge 1993
- Kurzweil 2005

* Russell & Norvig 2003, p. 963

[174] Transhumanism:

* Moravec 1988
* Kurzweil 2005
* Russell & Norvig 2003, p. 963

[175] AI as evolution:

* Edward Fredkin is quoted in McCorduck (2004, p. 401).
* Butler, Samuel (13 June 1863). *the Press* (Christchurch, New Zealand). http://www.nzetc.org/tm/scholarly/ tei-ButFir-t1-g1-t1-g1-t4-body.html, Letter to the Editor.
* Dyson, George (1998). *Darwin among the Machiens*. Allan Lane Science. ISBN 0738200301.

References

AI textbooks

* Luger, George; Stubblefield, William (2004). *Artificial Intelligence: Structures and Strategies for Complex Problem Solving* (http://www.cs.unm.edu/~luger/ai-final/tocfull.html) (5th ed.). The Benjamin/Cummings Publishing Company, Inc.. ISBN 0-8053-4780-1.
* Nilsson, Nils (1998). *Artificial Intelligence: A New Synthesis*. Morgan Kaufmann Publishers. ISBN 978-1-55860-467-4.
* Russell, Stuart J.; Norvig, Peter (2003), *Artificial Intelligence: A Modern Approach* (http://aima.cs.berkeley. edu/) (2nd ed.), Upper Saddle River, New Jersey: Prentice Hall, ISBN 0-13-790395-2
* Poole, David; Mackworth, Alan; Goebel, Randy (1998). *Computational Intelligence: A Logical Approach* (http:// www.cs.ubc.ca/spider/poole/ci.html). New York: Oxford University Press. ISBN 0195102703.
* Winston, Patrick Henry (1984). *Artificial Intelligence*. Reading, Massachusetts: Addison-Wesley. ISBN 0201082594.

History of AI

* Crevier, Daniel (1993), *AI: The Tumultuous Search for Artificial Intelligence*, New York, NY: BasicBooks, ISBN 0-465-02997-3
* McCorduck, Pamela (2004), *Machines Who Think* (http://www.pamelamc.com/html/machines_who_think. html) (2nd ed.), Natick, MA: A. K. Peters, Ltd., ISBN 1-56881-205-1

Nilsson, Nils (2010), The Quest for Artificial Intelligence: A History of Ideas and Achievements, New York, NY: Cambridge University Press, ISBN 978-0-52112-293

Other sources

* "ACM Computing Classification System: Artificial intelligence" (http://www.acm.org/class/1998/I.2.html). ACM. 1998. Retrieved 30 August 2007.
* Aleksander, Igor (1995). *Artificial Neuroconsciousness: An Update* (http://web.archive.org/web/ 19970302014628/http://www.ee.ic.ac.uk/research/neural/publications/iwann.html). IWANN. Archived from the original (http://www.ee.ic.ac.uk/research/neural/publications/iwann.html) on 2 March 1997. BibTex (http://dblp.uni-trier.de/rec/bibtex/conf/iwann/Aleksander95) Internet Archive (http://web.archive. org/web/19970302014628/http://www.ee.ic.ac.uk/research/neural/publications/iwann.html)
* Brooks, Rodney (1990). "Elephants Don't Play Chess" (http://people.csail.mit.edu/brooks/papers/elephants. pdf) (PDF). *Robotics and Autonomous Systems* **6**: 3–15. doi:10.1016/S0921-8890(05)80025-9. Retrieved 30 August 2007..
* Buchanan, Bruce G. (2005). "A (Very) Brief History of Artificial Intelligence" (http://www.aaai.org/AITopics/ assets/PDF/AIMag26-04-016.pdf) (PDF). *AI Magazine*: 53–60. Retrieved 30 August 2007.
* Dennett, Daniel (1991). *Consciousness Explained*. The Penguin Press. ISBN 0-7139-9037-6.

* Dreyfus, Hubert (1972). *What Computers Can't Do*. New York: MIT Press. ISBN 0060110821.
* Dreyfus, Hubert (1979). *What Computers Still Can't Do*. New York: MIT Press. ISBN 0262041340.
* Dreyfus, Hubert; Dreyfus, Stuart (1986). *Mind over Machine: The Power of Human Intuition and Expertise in the Era of the Computer*. Oxford, UK: Blackwell. ISBN 0029080606.
* Dreyfus, Hubert (1992). *What Computers Still Can't Do*. New York: MIT Press. ISBN 0-262-54067-3.
* Edelman, Gerald (23 November 2007). "Gerald Edelman – Neural Darwinism and Brain-based Devices" (http:// lis.epfl.ch/resources/podcast/2007/11/gerald-edelman-neural-darwinism-and.html). Talking Robots.
* Fearn, Nicholas (2007). *The Latest Answers to the Oldest Questions: A Philosophical Adventure with the World's Greatest Thinkers*. New York: Grove Press. ISBN 0802118399.
* Forster, Dion (2006). "Self validating consciousness in strong artificial intelligence: An African theological contribution" (http://www.spirituality.org.za/files/D Forster doctorate.pdf). Pretoria: University of South Africa.
* Gladwell, Malcolm (2005). *Blink*. New York: Little, Brown and Co.. ISBN 0-316-17232-4.
* Haugeland, John (1985). *Artificial Intelligence: The Very Idea*. Cambridge, Mass.: MIT Press. ISBN 0-262-08153-9.
* Hawkins, Jeff; Blakeslee, Sandra (2005). *On Intelligence*. New York, NY: Owl Books. ISBN 0-8050-7853-3.
* Hofstadter, Douglas (1979). *Gödel, Escher, Bach: an Eternal Golden Braid*. New York, NY: Vintage Books. ISBN 0394745027.
* Howe, J. (November 1994). "Artificial Intelligence at Edinburgh University: a Perspective" (http://www.inf.ed. ac.uk/about/AIhistory.html). Retrieved 30 August 2007..
* Kahneman, Daniel; Slovic, D.; Tversky, Amos (1982). *Judgment under uncertainty: Heuristics and biases*. New York: Cambridge University Press. ISBN 0521284147.
* Kolata, G. (1982). "How can computers get common sense?". *Science* **217** (4566): 1237–1238. doi:10.1126/science.217.4566.1237. PMID 17837639.
* Kurzweil, Ray (1999). *The Age of Spiritual Machines*. Penguin Books. ISBN 0-670-88217-8.
* Kurzweil, Ray (2005). *The Singularity is Near*. Penguin Books. ISBN 0-670-03384-7.
* Lakoff, George (1987). *Women, Fire, and Dangerous Things: What Categories Reveal About the Mind*. University of Chicago Press. ISBN 0-226-46804-6.
* Lakoff, George; Núñez, Rafael E. (2000). *Where Mathematics Comes From: How the Embodied Mind Brings Mathematics into Being*. Basic Books. ISBN 0-465-03771-2..
* Lenat, Douglas; Guha, R. V. (1989). *Building Large Knowledge-Based Systems*. Addison-Wesley. ISBN 0201517523.
* Lighthill, Professor Sir James (1973). "Artificial Intelligence: A General Survey". *Artificial Intelligence: a paper symposium*. Science Research Council.
* Lucas, John (1961). "Minds, Machines and Gödel" (http://users.ox.ac.uk/~jrlucas/Godel/mmg.html). In Anderson, A.R.. *Minds and Machines*. Retrieved 30 August 2007.
* Maker, Meg Houston (2006). "AI@50: AI Past, Present, Future" (http://www.engagingexperience.com/2006/ 07/ai50_ai_past_pr.html). Dartmouth College. Retrieved 16 October 2008.
* McCarthy, John; Minsky, Marvin; Rochester, Nathan; Shannon, Claude (1955). "A Proposal for the Dartmouth Summer Research Project on Artificial Intelligence" (http://www-formal.stanford.edu/jmc/history/dartmouth/ dartmouth.html). Retrieved 30 August 2007..
* McCarthy, John; Hayes, P. J. (1969). "Some philosophical problems from the standpoint of artificial intelligence" (http://www-formal.stanford.edu/jmc/mcchay69.html). *Machine Intelligence* **4**: 463–502. Retrieved 30 August 2007.
* McCarthy, John (12 November 2007). "What Is Artificial Intelligence?" (http://www-formal.stanford.edu/jmc/ whatisai/whatisai.html).

- Minsky, Marvin (1967). *Computation: Finite and Infinite Machines*. Englewood Cliffs, N.J.: Prentice-Hall. ISBN 0131654497.
- Minsky, Marvin (2006). *The Emotion Machine*. New York, NY: Simon & Schusterl. ISBN 0-7432-7663-9.
- Moravec, Hans (1976). "The Role of Raw Power in Intelligence" (http://www.frc.ri.cmu.edu/users/hpm/ project.archive/general.articles/1975/Raw.Power.html). Retrieved 30 August 2007.
- Moravec, Hans (1988). *Mind Children*. Harvard University Press. ISBN 0674576160.
- NRC, (United States National Research Council) (1999). "Developments in Artificial Intelligence". *Funding a Revolution: Government Support for Computing Research*. National Academy Press.
- Needham, Joseph (1986). *Science and Civilization in China: Volume 2*. Caves Books Ltd..
- Newell, Allen; Simon, H. A. (1963). "GPS: A Program that Simulates Human Thought". In Feigenbaum, E.A.; Feldman, J.. *Computers and Thought*. New York: McGraw-Hill.
- Newell, Allen; Simon, H. A. (1976). "Computer Science as Empirical Inquiry: Symbols and Search" (http:// www.rci.rutgers.edu/~cfs/472_html/AI_SEARCH/PSS/PSSH4.html). *Communications of the ACM*. **19**..
- Tecuci, Gheorghe (2011). "Artificial Intelligence" (http://bf4dv7zn3u.search.serialssolutions.com.myaccess. library.utoronto.ca/?ctx_ver=Z39.88-2004&ctx_enc=info:ofi/enc:UTF-8&rfr_id=info:sid/summon. serialssolutions.com&rft_val_fmt=info:ofi/fmt:kev:mtx:journal&rft.genre=article&rft.atitle=Artificial+ intelligence&rft.jtitle=Wiley+Interdisciplinary+Reviews:+Computational+Statistics&rft.au=Tecuci,+ Gheorghe&rft.date=2012-03-01&rft.pub=John+Wiley+&+Sons,+Inc&rft.issn=1939-5108&rft. volume=4&rft.issue=2&rft.spage=168&rft.epage=180&rft_id=info:doi/10.1002/wics.200&rft. externalDocID=WICS200). *artificial intelligence*..
- Nilsson, Nils (1983), "Artificial Intelligence Prepares for 2001" (http://ai.stanford.edu/~nilsson/ OnlinePubs-Nils/General Essays/AIMag04-04-002.pdf), *AI Magazine* **1** (1), Presidential Address to the Association for the Advancement of Artificial Intelligence.
- Penrose, Roger (1989). *The Emperor's New Mind: Concerning Computer, Minds and The Laws of Physics*. Oxford University Press. ISBN 0-198-51973-7.
- Searle, John (1980). "Minds, Brains and Programs" (http://www.bbsonline.org/documents/a/00/00/04/84/ bbs00000484-00/bbs.searle2.html). *Behavioral and Brain Sciences* **3** (3): 417–457. doi:10.1017/S0140525X00005756.
- Searle, John (1999). *Mind, language and society*. New York, NY: Basic Books. ISBN 0465045219. OCLC 231867665 43689264.
- Serenko, Alexander; Detlor, Brian (2004). "Intelligent agents as innovations" (http://foba.lakeheadu.ca/ serenko/papers/Serenko_Detlor_AI_and_Society.pdf). *AI and Society* **18** (4): 364–381. doi:10.1007/s00146-004-0310-5.
- Serenko, Alexander; Ruhi, Umar; Cocosila, Mihail (2007). "Unplanned effects of intelligent agents on Internet use: Social Informatics approach" (http://foba.lakeheadu.ca/serenko/papers/ AI_Society_Serenko_Social_Impacts_of_Agents.pdf). *AI and Society* **21** (1–2): 141–166. doi:10.1007/s00146-006-0051-8.
- Shapiro, Stuart C. (1992). "Artificial Intelligence" (http://www.cse.buffalo.edu/~shapiro/Papers/ai.pdf). In Shapiro, Stuart C.. *Encyclopedia of Artificial Intelligence* (2nd ed.). New York: John Wiley. pp. 54–57. ISBN 0471503061.
- Simon, H. A. (1965). *The Shape of Automation for Men and Management*. New York: Harper & Row.
- Skillings, Jonathan (3 July 2006). "Getting Machines to Think Like Us" (http://news.cnet.com/ Getting-machines-to-think-like-us/2008-11394_3-6090207.html). *cnet*. Retrieved 3 February 2011.
- Turing, Alan (October 1950), "Computing Machinery and Intelligence" (http://loebner.net/Prizef/ TuringArticle.html), *Mind* **LIX** (236): 433–460, doi:10.1093/mind/LIX.236.433, ISSN 0026-4423, retrieved 2008-08-18.

- van der Walt, Christiaan; Bernard, Etienne (2006<!—year is presumed based on acknowledgements at the end of the article—>). "Data characteristics that determine classifier performance" (http://www.patternrecognition.co.za/publications/cvdwalt_data_characteristics_classifiers.pdf) (PDF). Retrieved 5 August 2009.
- Vinge, Vernor (1993). "The Coming Technological Singularity: How to Survive in the Post-Human Era" (http://www-rohan.sdsu.edu/faculty/vinge/misc/singularity.html).
- Wason, P. C.; Shapiro, D. (1966). "Reasoning". In Foss, B. M.. *New horizons in psychology*. Harmondsworth: Penguin.
- Weizenbaum, Joseph (1976). *Computer Power and Human Reason*. San Francisco: W.H. Freeman & Company. ISBN 0716704641.
- Tecuci, Gheorghe (2012). "Artificial intelligence" (http://bf4dv7zn3u.search.serialssolutions.com.myaccess.library.utoronto.ca/?ctx_ver=Z39.88-2004&ctx_enc=info:ofi/enc:UTF-8&rfr_id=info:sid/summon.serialssolutions.com&rft_val_fmt=info:ofi/fmt:kev:mtx:journal&rft.genre=article&rft.atitle=Artificial+intelligence&rft.jtitle=Wiley+Interdisciplinary+Reviews:+Computational+Statistics&rft.au=Tecuci,+Gheorghe&rft.date=2012-03-01&rft.pub=John+Wiley+&+Sons,+Inc&rft.issn=1939-5108&rft.volume=4&rft.issue=2&rft.spage=168&rft.epage=180&rft_id=info:doi/10.1002/wics.200&rft.externalDocID=WICS200).

Further reading

- TechCast Article Series, John Sagi, Framing Consciousness (http://www.techcast.org/Upload/PDFs/634146249446122137_Consciousness-Sagifinalversion.pdf)
- Boden, Margaret, Mind As Machine, Oxford University Press, 2006
- Johnston, John (2008) "The Allure of Machinic Life: Cybernetics, Artificial Life, and the New AI", MIT Press
- Myers, Courtney Boyd ed. (2009). The AI Report (http://www.forbes.com/2009/06/22/singularity-robots-computers-opinions-contributors-artificial-intelligence-09_land.html). Forbes June 2009
- Serenko, Alexander (2010). "The development of an AI journal ranking based on the revealed preference approach" (http://foba.lakeheadu.ca/serenko/papers/JOI_Serenko_AI_Journal_Ranking_Published.pdf) (PDF). *Journal of Informetrics* **4** (4): 447–459. doi:10.1016/j.joi.2010.04.001.
- Sun, R. & Bookman, L. (eds.), *Computational Architectures: Integrating Neural and Symbolic Processes*. Kluwer Academic Publishers, Needham, MA. 1994.

External links

- What Is AI? (http://www-formal.stanford.edu/jmc/whatisai/whatisai.html) — An introduction to artificial intelligence by AI founder John McCarthy.
- Logic and Artificial Intelligence (http://plato.stanford.edu/entries/logic-ai) entry by Richmond Thomason in the *Stanford Encyclopedia of Philosophy*
- AI (http://www.dmoz.org/Computers/Artificial_Intelligence//) at the Open Directory Project
- AITopics (http://aaai.org/AITopics/) — A large directory of links and other resources maintained by the Association for the Advancement of Artificial Intelligence, the leading organization of academic AI researchers.
- Artificial Intelligence Discussion group (https://www.researchgate.net/group/Artificial_Intelligence)

Community_network

Community network is a term used broadly to indicate the use of networking technologies by, and for, a local community. Free-nets and civic networks indicate roughly the same range of projects and services, whereas community technology centers (CTCs) and telecentres generally indicate a physical facility to compensate for lack of access to information and communication technologies (ICTs).

Although there is no absolute agreement on the definition of the term, it is generally agreed that a community network is a computer-based system that is intended to help support geographical communities by supporting, augmenting, and extending already existing social networks.

Function

Community networks often provide free web space, e-mail, and other services for free, without advertising. VillageSoup launched a distinct form of community networking in 1997. This form uses display ads and informational postings from fee-paying business and organization members to generate revenue critical to the support of professional journalists producing news for the community.

Community network organizations often engage in training and other services and sometimes are involved in policy work. The Seattle Community Network is a prominent example.

When one looks at the entries of community network directories or the papers and Web sites whose titles and names include "community network" or "community networking," it is noticeable that a variety of practices exist. This diversity can be seen in the types of information and services offered, who operates the network, and the area covered.

The most extensive array of information services in a community network includes news from professional and amateur reporters, news and information from businesses and organizations; community events listings; weather forecasts; listings of governmental offices, businesses and organizations; and galleries of images of the place. Services include requesting alerts and RSS feeds; making reservations; searching for goods and services; purchasing images and auction items; and posting personal and commercial advertisements. A printed periodic publication is sometimes a service of the community network.

Some community networks limit themselves to functions such as facilitating communication among non-profit organizations.

Internet-based volunteer networks of blogs and groups have been formed in the internet social-networking field as well. The Alabama Charity Network for example provides another place for people to connect to fundraisers and charity information using internet-based social networking.

The entities in charge of planning and operating the community networks may be government offices, chambers of commerce, public libraries, non-profit organizations, for-profit entities or volunteer groups.

The primary goals of a community network may include providing a sustainable, trusted platform for an urban neighborhood, suburban village or exurban town or region to enhance a vital community and functioning democracy; closing of the digital divide across socio-economic lines; offering easier access to already existing information and services; promotion of local economic development and employment; strengthening of local identity; and/or revitalization, promotion, and/or maintenance of local communal ties.

The area identified with a community network could be a town, city, county, metropolitan neighborhood, state, and occasionally a region.

History

Among the earliest practices that are frequently mentioned are Big Sky Telegraph (Montana, USA), Cleveland Free-Net (Cleveland, USA) Public Electronic Network (PEN) in Santa Monica (California, USA), Digital Stad in Amsterdam (The Netherlands) [1].

Bryggenet is a community network in Copenhagen, Denmark.

Fox Cities Online [2] (FOCOL) is a community network in the Fox Cities region of Wisconsin that has been in operation since the early 1990s.

VillageSoup[3] created the first community network based on a business model suggested in the 1997 book Net Gain: Expanding Markets Through Virtual Communities, authored by John Hagel III and Arthur G. Armstrong, two Mckinsey & Company, Inc. consultants.

References

- Schuler, Douglas. (1996) New Community Networks: Wired for Change [4]. Reading, MA: Addison-Wesley.

External links

- Free Culture, Free Software, Free Infrastructures! [5] : Interviews with Kloschi, Jürgen Neumann (Freifunk Germany), Kurt Jansson (Wikimedia Germany), Rishab Aiyer Ghosh (United Nations University), Lawrence Lessig (Creative Commons), Allison, Benoit (Montréal Wireless Community)]
- Alabama Charity Network (Alabama charity network blog) [6]

Wikibooks

- Information and Communication Technologies for Poverty Alleviation [7]

References

[1] http://www.scn.org/ncn/
[2] http://www.focol.org/
[3] http://www.villagesoup.com
[4] http://www.publicsphereproject.org/ncn/
[5] http://perspektive89.com/2006/10/18/
    free_culture_free_software_free_infrastructures_openness_and_freedom_in_every_layer_of_the_network_flo_fleissig_episo
[6] http://alabamacharity.wordpress.com
[7] http://en.wikibooks.org/wiki/Information_and_Communication_Technologies_for_Poverty_Alleviation/

Communications of the ACM

Editor-in-chief	Moshe Y. Vardi
Categories	Computer Science
Frequency	Monthly
First issue	1957
Company	Association for Computing Machinery
Country	United States
Language	English
Website	http://cacm.acm.org
ISSN	0001-0782 [1]

Communications of the ACM (*CACM*) is the monthly journal of the Association for Computing Machinery (ACM). Established in 1957, CACM is sent to all ACM members, currently numbering about 80,000. The articles are intended for readers with backgrounds in all areas of computer science and information systems. The focus is on the practical implications of advances in information technology and associated management issues; ACM also publishes a variety of more theoretical journals.

CACM straddles the boundary of a science magazine, professional journal, and a scientific journal. While the content is subject to peer review (and is counted as such in many university assessments of research output), the articles published are often summaries of research that may also be published elsewhere. Material published must be accessible and relevant to a broad readership. On the publisher's website, CACM is filed in the category "magazines". [2]

Influential articles

Many of the great debates and results in computing history have been published in the pages of *CACM*. Examples include:

- The issue of what to call the then-fledgling field of computer science was raised by the editors of DATA-LINK in a letter to the editor of CACM, appearing in 1958, the first year of CACM. They called for giving the field a name "which is brief, definite, distinctive". [3] The call was echoed by a wide range of suggestions, including *comptology* (Quentin Correll), [4] *hypology* (P.A. Zaphyr), [5] and *datalogy* (Peter Naur). [6]
- C. A. R. Hoare's Quicksort. [7]
- Martin Davis, George Logemann and Donald Loveland described in 1962 the DPLL algorithm, containing the essential algorithm on which most modern SAT solvers are based. [8]
- The "Revised report on the algorithm language ALGOL 60": A landmark paper in programming language design describing the result of the international ALGOL committee. [9]
- The issue of changing ACM's name, since the "machinery" in question is no longer the size of a house and is now measured in micrometres. [10] [11] [12]
- Kristen Nygaard and Ole-Johan Dahl's original paper on Simula-67. [13]
- Edsger W. Dijkstra's famous letter inveighing against the use of GOTO. [14] The letter was reprinted in Jan 2008 in the 60th anniversary edition of *CACM*. [15]
- Dijkstra's original paper on the THE operating system. This paper's appendix, arguably even more influential than its main body, introduced semaphore-based synchronization. [16]
- Ronald L. Rivest, Adi Shamir, and Leonard M. Adleman's first public-key cryptosystem (RSA). [17]

See also

- *Journal of the ACM*

References

[1] http://www.worldcat.org/issn/0001-0782

[2] "Publications — Association for Computing Machinery" (http://www.acm.org/publications). Acm.org. . Retrieved 2011-12-05.

[3] Weiss, E. A.; Corley, Henry P. T. (1958). "Letters to the editor". *Communications of the ACM* **1** (4): 6. doi:10.1145/368796.368802.

[4] *Communications of the ACM* **1** (7): 2.

[5] *Communications of the ACM* **2** (1): 4.

[6] *Communications of the ACM* **9** (7): 485.

[7] C.A.R. Hoare (1961). "Partition: Algorithm 63, Quicksort: Algorithm 64, and Find: Algorithm 65". *Communications of the ACM* **4** (7): 321.

[8] M. Davis, G. Logemann, D. Loveland (1962). "A Machine Program for Theorem Proving". *Communications of the ACM* **5** (7): 394. doi:10.1145/368273.368557.

[9] Backus, J. W.; Wegstein, J. H.; Van Wijngaarden, A.; Woodger, M.; Nauer, P.; Bauer, F. L.; Green, J.; Katz, C. et al (1963). "Revised report on the algorithm language ALGOL 60". *Communications of the ACM* **6** (1): 1. doi:10.1145/366193.366201.

[10] G.E. Forsythe (1965). "President's letter to the ACM membership: Why ACM?". *Communications of the ACM* **8** (7): 422. doi:10.1145/364995.364997.

[11] D.D. McCracken (1976). "A letter from the ACM Vice-President: The ACM name change". *Communications of the ACM* **19** (10): 539. doi:10.1145/360349.360351. In this letter, McCracken suggests that the word *machinery* is dropped from the name. To highlight the seriousness of the situation, he writes: "If we don't act *sometime*, we'll still be called Association for Computing Machinery in the year 2000."

[12] R.L. Ashenhurst (1986). "ACM forum". *Communications of the ACM* **29** (4): 260–265. doi:10.1145/5684.315614.. A letter by P.A.T. Wolfgang ("I thought that the name issue died in 1978") and responses by R.L. Ashenhurst and R.F. Hespos.

[13] K. Nygaard, O.-J. Dahl (1966). "Simula: An ALGOL-based simulation language". *Communications of the ACM* **9** (9): 671. doi:10.1145/365813.365819.

[14] E.W. Dijkstra (1968). "Go To statement considered harmful". *Communications of the ACM* **11** (3): 148.

[15] E.W. Dijkstra (2008 [1968]). "(A Look Back at) Go To Statement Considered Harmful" (http://mags.acm.org/communications/200801/?pg=9). Association for Computing Machinery. . Retrieved 2008-06-12.

[16] E.W. Dijkstra (1968). "Structure of the 'THE'-Multiprogramming System". *Communications of the ACM* **11** (5): 341. doi:10.1145/363095.363143.

[17] R.L. Rivest, A. Shamir, L.M. Adleman (1978). "A Method for Obtaining Digital Signatures and Public-Key Cryptosystems". *Communications of the ACM* **21** (2): 120. doi:10.1145/359340.359342.

External links

- Official website (http://http://cacm.acm.org)
- ISSN 0001-0782

Barbara_Simons

Barbara Simons (born 1941) is a computer scientist and past president of the Association for Computing Machinery (ACM). She has held various technical, administrative, and public policy positions with the ACM since the early 1990s [1]; she is founder and former Chair of USACM, the ACM U.S. Public Policy Committee. Her main areas of research are compiler optimization and scheduling theory. Together with Douglas W. Jones, in Spring 2012 Simons will be publishing a book on electronic voting entitled Ballots: Will Your Vote Count? [2] [3]

Barbara Simons

After receiving her Ph.D. in 1981 in computer science from the University of California, Berkeley, she joined the Research Division of IBM, from which she took early retirement in 1998. In 1992, *Science* featured her in a special edition on women in science. In 2005 Simons became the first woman to receive the Distinguished Engineering Alumni Award from the College of Engineering of U.C. Berkeley.

She served on the President's Export Council's Subcommittee on Encryption and on the Information Technology-Sector of the President's Council on the Year 2000 Conversion. She is on the Board of Directors of VerifiedVoting.org. She has also been on the boards of the U. C. Berkeley Engineering Fund, the Electronic Privacy Information Center, Public Knowledge, and the Oxford Internet Institute, as well as the Advisory Council of the Public Interest Registry's ORG. She has testified before both the U.S. and state legislatures and at government sponsored hearings. She was runner-up in the first (and only) election for the North America seat on the ICANN Board.

Simons co-founded the Reentry Program for Women and Minorities in the Computer Science Department at U.C. Berkeley. She is also on the Boards of the Coalition to Diversify Computing (CDC) and the Berkeley Foundation for Opportunities in Information Technology (BFOIT), groups that work at increasing participation in computer science of women and underrepresented minorities.

Since at least 2002 Simons has been a critic of unauditable electronic voting and is generally credited as a key player in getting the League of Women Voters to change its stance on this issue. Initially the League had seen electronic voting mainly as a way to minimize invalidly cast ballots, but at their June 2004 convention she led a successful fight to get this policy reversed to one of giving priority to voting machines that are "recountable".[4]

She was a member of the National Workshop on Internet Voting that was convened at the request of President Clinton and produced a report on Internet Voting in 2001. She also participated on the Security Peer Review Group for the US Department of Defense's Internet voting project (SERVE) and co-authored the report that led to the cancellation of SERVE because of security concerns.[5] [6] Simons co-chaired the ACM study of statewide databases of registered voters.[7] She recently co-authored the League of Women Voters report on election auditing.[8] In 2008 she was appointed to the Election Assistance Commission Board of Advisors by Senator Harry Reid.

She is divorced from James Harris Simons, a mathematician and hedge fund manager. In 1996, their son Paul, age 34, was killed by a car while riding a bicycle near the Simons home.

Awards and honors

- CPSR Norbert Wiener Award for Professional and Social Responsibility in Computing (1992)
- ACM Fellow (1993)
- American Association for the Advancement of Science Fellow (1993)
- Named by *Open Computing* as one of the top 100 women in computing
- Selected by CNET as one of 26 Internet "Visionaries" (1995)
- Electronic Frontier Foundation Pioneer Award (1998)
- U. C. Berkeley Computer Science Department Distinguished Alumnus Award in Computer Science and Engineering (2000)
- ACM Outstanding Contribution Award (2002)
- Computing Research Association Distinguished Service Award (2004)
- University of California, Berkeley College of Engineering Distinguished Engineering Alumni Award (2005)
- U.S. Election Assistance Commission Board of Advisors (2008)

See also

- James Harris Simons

References

[1] http://www.iwt.org/whoweare/bios/barbarasimonsbio.html

[2] http://brokenballots.com/"Broken

[3] Douglas W. Jones and Barbara Simons, Broken Ballots (http://www.press.uchicago.edu/ucp/books/book/distributed/B/bo13383590.
html), Center for the Study of Language and Information / University of Chicago Press, 2012.

[4] Ronnie Dugger, "How They Could Steal the Election This Time", *The Nation*, p.13 August 16/23, 2004

[5] David Jefferson, Aviel D. Rubin, Barbara Simons and David Wagner, A Security Analysis of the Secure Electronic Registration and Voting
Experiment (SERVE) (http://servesecurityreport.org/paper.pdf), Jan. 20, 2004.

[6] Press Release, [Pentagon Decides Against Internet Voting http://www.defense.gov/news/newsarticle.aspx?id=27362], American Forces
Press Service, Feb. 6, 2004.

[7] Paula Hawthorn and Barbara Simons (co-chairs), Statewide Databases of Registered Voters: Study Of Accuracy, Privacy, Usability, Security,
and Reliability Issues (http://usacm.acm.org/images/documents/vrd_report2.pdf), U.S. Public Policy Committee of the Association for
Computing Machinery, Feb. 2006.

[8] Eleciton Audits Task Force, Report on Election Auditing (http://verifiedvoting.org/downloads/Report_ElectionAudits.pdf), League of
Women Voters of the United States, Jan. 2009.

External links

- Works by or about Barbara Simons (http://worldcat.org/identities/lccn-n90-693747) in libraries (WorldCat catalog)

Douglas_Engelbart

<table>
<tr><td colspan="2" align="center">Douglas Carl Engelbart ("Doug")</td></tr>
<tr><td colspan="2" align="center">
Douglas Engelbart in 2008</td></tr>
<tr><td>Born</td><td>January 30, 1925Portland, Oregon, USA</td></tr>
<tr><td>Citizenship</td><td>US</td></tr>
<tr><td>Nationality</td><td>US</td></tr>
<tr><td>Fields</td><td>Inventor</td></tr>
<tr><td>Institutions</td><td>Stanford Research Institute, Tymshare, McDonnell Douglas, Bootstrap Institute/Alliance [1], Doug Engelbart Institute [2]</td></tr>
<tr><td>Alma mater</td><td>Oregon State College (BS); UC Berkeley (PhD)</td></tr>
<tr><td>Doctoral advisor</td><td>John R. Woodyard</td></tr>
<tr><td>Known for</td><td>Computer mouse, Hypertext, Groupware, Interactive Computing</td></tr>
<tr><td>Notable awards</td><td>National Medal of Technology, Lemelson-MIT Prize, Turing Award, Lovelace Medal, Norbert Wiener Award for Social and Professional Responsibility, Fellow Award, Computer History Museum [3]</td></tr>
<tr><td colspan="2" align="center">Website</td></tr>
<tr><td colspan="2" align="center">dougengelbart.org [2]</td></tr>
</table>

Douglas Carl Engelbart (born January 30, 1925) is an American inventor, and an early computer and internet pioneer. He is best known for his work on the challenges of human-computer interaction, resulting in the invention of the computer mouse,[4] and the development of hypertext, networked computers, and precursors to GUIs. He is a committed, vocal proponent of the development and use of computers and networks to help cope with the world's increasingly urgent and complex problems.[5]

Engelbart embedded a set of organizing principles in his lab, which he termed "bootstrapping strategy". He designed the strategy to accelerate the rate of innovation of his lab.[6]

Early life and education

Engelbart was born in Portland, Oregon on January 30, 1925 to Carl Louis Engelbart and Gladys Charlotte Amelia Munson Engelbart. He is of German, Swedish and Norwegian descent.[7]

He was the middle of three children, with a sister Dorianne (3 years older), and a brother David (14 months younger). They lived in Portland in his early years, and moved to the countryside to Johnson Creek when he was 9 or 10, after the death of his father. He graduated from Portland's Franklin High School in 1942.

Midway through his college studies at Oregon State University (then called Oregon State College), near the end of World War II, he was drafted into the US Navy, serving two years as a radar technician in the Philippines. On a small island, in a tiny hut on stilts, he first read Vannevar Bush's article "As We May Think", which greatly inspired him.

He returned to Oregon State and completed his Bachelor's degree in electrical engineering in 1948.

While at Oregon State, he was a member of Sigma Phi Epsilon social fraternity. He was hired by the National Advisory Committee for Aeronautics at the Ames Research Center, where he worked through 1951.[8]

Career and accomplishments

Epiphany

Doug Engelbart's career was inspired in 1951 when he got engaged and suddenly realized he had no career goals beyond getting a good education and a decent job. Over several months he reasoned that:

The first prototype of a computer mouse, as designed by Bill English from Engelbart's sketches[9]

1. he would focus his career on making the world a better place;
2. any serious effort to make the world better requires some kind of organized effort;
3. harnessing the collective human intellect of all the people contributing to effective solutions was the key;
4. if you could dramatically improve how we do that, you'd be boosting every effort on the planet to solve important problems - the sooner the better; and
5. computers could be the vehicle for dramatically improving this capability.

In 1945, Engelbart had read with interest Vannevar Bush's article "As We May Think",[10] a call to arms for making knowledge widely available as a national peacetime grand challenge. Doug had also read something about computers (a relatively recent phenomenon), and from his experience as a radar technician he knew that information could be analyzed and displayed on a screen. He envisioned intellectual workers sitting at display 'working stations', flying through information space, harnessing their collective intellectual capacity to solve important problems together in much more powerful ways. Harnessing collective intellect, facilitated by interactive computers, became his life's mission at a time when computers were viewed as number crunching tools.

He enrolled in graduate school in electrical engineering at University of California, Berkeley, graduating with an MS degree in 1953, and a Ph.D. in 1955.[8] As a graduate student at Berkeley he assisted in the construction of the California Digital Computer project CALDIC. His graduate work led to several patents.[11] After completing his PhD he stayed on at Berkeley as assistant professor to teach for a year, and left when it was clear he could not pursue his vision there. He then formed a startup, Digital Techniques, to commercialize some of his doctorate research on storage devices, but after a year decided instead to pursue the research he had been dreaming of since 1951. He took a position at Stanford Research Institute (SRI) in Menlo Park, in 1957. He initially worked for Hewitt Crane on magnetic devices and miniaturization of electronics; Engelbart and Crane became lifelong friends.

SRI and ARC

At SRI, Engelbart gradually obtained over a dozen patents (some resulting from his graduate work), and by 1962 produced a report about his vision and proposed research agenda titled *Augmenting Human Intellect: A Conceptual Framework*.[12] This led to funding from ARPA to launch his work. Engelbart recruited a research team in his new Augmentation Research Center (ARC, the lab he founded at SRI), and became the driving force behind the design and development of the On-Line System, or NLS. He and his team developed computer-interface elements such as bit-mapped screens, the mouse, hypertext, collaborative tools, and precursors to the graphical user interface. He conceived and developed many of his user interface ideas back in the mid-1960s, long before the personal computer revolution, at a time when most individuals were kept away from computers, and could only use computers through intermediaries (see batch processing), and when software tended to be written for vertical applications in proprietary systems.

Engelbart applied for a patent in 1967 and received it in 1970, for the wooden shell with two metal wheels (computer mouse - U.S. Patent 3541541 [13]), which he had developed with Bill English, his lead engineer, a few years earlier. In the patent application it is described as an *"X-Y position indicator for a display system"*. Engelbart later revealed that it was nicknamed the "mouse" because the tail came out the end. His group also called the on-screen cursor a "bug", but this term was not widely adopted.

Two Apple Macintosh Plus mice, 1986

He never received any royalties for his mouse invention. During an interview, he says "SRI patented the mouse, but they really had no idea of its value. Some years later it was learned that they had licensed it to Apple for something like $40,000."

Engelbart showcased the chorded keyboard and many more of his and ARC's inventions in 1968 at the so-called mother of all demos.[14]

ARPANET

Engelbart's research was funded by ARPA, SRI's ARC became involved with the ARPANET (the precursor of the Internet).

The first message on the ARPANET was sent by UCLA student programmer Charley Kline, at 10:30 p.m, on October 29, 1969 from Boelter Hall 3420.[15] Supervised by Kleinrock, Kline transmitted from the university's SDS Sigma 7 Host computer to the Stanford Research Institute's SDS 940 Host computer. The message text was the word "login"; the "l" and the "o" letters were transmitted, but the system then crashed. Hence, the literal first message over the ARPANET was "lo". About an hour later, having recovered from the crash, the SDS Sigma 7 computer effected a full "login". The first permanent ARPANET link was established on November 21, 1969, between the IMP at UCLA and the IMP at the Stanford Research Institute. By December 5, 1969, the entire four-node network was established.[16]

In addition to SRI and UCLA, UCSB, and the University of Utah were part of the original four network nodes. By December 5, 1969, the entire 4-node network was connected.

ARC soon became the first Network Information Center and thus managed the directory for connections among all ARPANET nodes. ARC also published a large percentage of the early Request For Comments, an ongoing series of publications that document the evolution of ARPANET into the Internet. Although the NIC at first used NLS, it was intended to be a production service to other network users, while Engelbart continued to focus on innovative research. This inherent conflict led to establishing the NIC as its own group, led by Elizabeth J. Feinler.[17]

Anecdotal notes

Historian of science Thierry Bardini argues that Engelbart's complex personal philosophy (which drove all his research) foreshadowed the modern application of the concept of coevolution to the philosophy and use of technology.[18]

Bardini points out that Engelbart was strongly influenced by the principle of linguistic relativity developed by Benjamin Lee Whorf. Where Whorf reasoned that the sophistication of a language controls the sophistication of the thoughts that can be expressed by a speaker of that language, Engelbart reasoned that the state of our current technology controls our ability to manipulate information, and that fact in turn will control our ability to develop new, improved technologies. He thus set himself to the revolutionary task of developing computer-based technologies for manipulating information directly, and also to improve individual and group processes for knowledge-work.[18]

End of research career

Engelbart slipped into relative obscurity after 1976. Several of Engelbart's researchers became alienated from him and left his organization for Xerox PARC, in part due to frustration, and in part due to differing views of the future of computing. Engelbart saw the future in collaborative, networked, timeshare (client-server) computers, which younger programmers rejected in favor of the personal computer. The conflict was both technical and social: the younger programmers came from an era where centralized power was highly suspect, and personal computing was just barely on the horizon.

Engelbart served on the board of directors of Erhard Seminars Training. Several key ARC personnel were also involved. Although EST had been recommended by other researchers, the controversial nature of EST and other social experiments reduced the morale and social cohesion of the ARC community.[18]

The Mansfield Amendment, the end of the Vietnam War, and the end of the Apollo program reduced ARC's funding from ARPA and NASA. SRI's management, which disapproved of Engelbart's approach to running the center, placed the remains of ARC under the control of artificial intelligence researcher Bertram Raphael, who negotiated the transfer of the laboratory to a company called Tymshare. Engelbart's house in Atherton burned down during this period, causing him and his family even further problems. Tymshare took over NLS and the lab that Engelbart had founded, hired most of the lab's staff including its creator as a Senior Scientist, renamed the software *Augment*, and offered it as a commercial service via its new Office Automation Division. Tymshare was already somewhat familiar with NLS; back when ARC was still operational, it had experimented with its own local copy of the NLS software on a minicomputer called OFFICE-1, as part of a joint project with ARC.

At Tymshare, Engelbart soon found himself marginalized and relegated to obscurity. Operational concerns at Tymshare overrode Engelbart's desire to do further research. Various executives, first at Tymshare and later at McDonnell Douglas (which took over Tymshare in 1984), expressed interest in his ideas, but never committed the funds or the people to further develop them. His interest inside of McDonnell Douglas was focused on the enormous knowledge management and IT requirements involved in the lifecycle of an aerospace program, which served to strengthen Doug's resolve to motivate the IT arena toward global interoperability and an open hyperdocument system.[19] Engelbart retired from McDonnell Douglas in 1986, determined pursue his work free from commercial pressure.

Teaming with his daughter, Christina Engelbart, in 1988 he founded the Bootstrap Institute to coalesce his ideas into a series of three-day and half-day management seminars offered at Stanford University 1989–2000. By the early 1990s there was sufficient interest among his seminar graduates to launch a collaborative implementation of his work, and the Bootstrap Alliance was formed as a non-profit home base for this effort. Although the invasion of Iraq and subsequent recession spawned a rash of belt-tightening reorganizations which drastically redirected the efforts of their alliance partners, they continued with the management seminars, consulting, and small-scale collaborations. In the mid-1990s they were awarded some DARPA funding to develop a modern user interface to Augment, called Visual AugTerm (VAT), while participating in a larger program addressing the IT requirements of the Joint Task Force.

Honors

Since the late 1980s, prominent individuals and organizations have recognized the seminal importance of Engelbart's contributions:[20]

In December 1995, at the Fourth WWW Conference in Boston, he was the first recipient of what would later become the Yuri Rubinsky Memorial Award. In 1997 he was awarded the Lemelson-MIT Prize of $500,000, the world's largest single prize for invention and innovation, and the ACM Turing Award. To mark the 30th anniversary of Engelbart's 1968 demo, in 1998 the Stanford Silicon Valley Archives [21] and the Institute for the Future hosted *Engelbart's Unfinished Revolution*[22], a symposium at Stanford University's Memorial Auditorium, to honor Engelbart and his ideas. Also that year, ACM SIGCHI awarded him the CHI Lifetime Achievement Award (and inducted him into the CHI Academy in 2002).

Engelbart was awarded The Franklin Institute's Certificate of Merit in 1996 and the Benjamin Franklin Medal in 1999 in Computer and Cognitive Science.

In early 2000 Engelbart produced, with volunteers and sponsors, what was called *The Unfinished Revolution — II*[23], also known as the *Engelbart Colloquium* at Stanford University, to document and publicize his work and ideas to a larger audience (live, and online).[24] [25]

In December 2000, US President Bill Clinton awarded Engelbart the National Medal of Technology, the United States' highest technology award.[26] In 2001 he was awarded a British Computer Society's Lovelace Medal, and in 2005 he was made a Fellow of the Computer History Museum and honored with the Norbert Wiener Award, which is given annually by Computer Professionals for Social Responsibility.

Robert X. Cringely did an hour long interview with Engelbart on December 9, 2005 in his NerdTV [27] video podcast series. On December 9, 2008, Engelbart was honored at the 40th Anniversary celebration of the 1968 "Mother of All Demos".[28] This event, produced by SRI International, was held at Memorial Auditorium at Stanford University. Speakers included several members of Engelbart's original Augmentation Research Center (ARC) team including Don Andrews, Bill Paxton, Bill English, and Jeff Rulifson, Engelbart's chief government sponsor Bob Taylor, and other pioneers of interactive computing, including Andy van Dam and Alan Kay. In addition, Christina Engelbart spoke about her father's early influences and the ongoing work of the Doug Engelbart Institute.[29] In June 2009, the New Media Consortium recognized Engelbart as an NMC Fellow [30] for his lifetime of achievements. In 2011, Engelbart was inducted into IEEE Intelligent Systems' AI's Hall of Fame.[31] [32]

Recent work and legacy

Doug Engelbart attended Program for the Future 2010 Conference[33] where hundreds of people convened at The Tech Museum in San Jose and online to engage in dialog about how to pursue Doug Engelbart's vision to augment collective intelligence.

The most complete coverage of Engelbart's bootstrapping ideas can be found in *Boosting Our Collective IQ*,[34] by Douglas C. Engelbart, 1995. This is a special keepsake including three of Engelbart's key papers, artfully edited and produced into book form by Yuri Rubinsky and Christina Engelbart to commemorate the presentation of the 1995 SoftQuad Web Award to Doug Engelbart at the World Wide Web conference in Boston that December, honoring his early and seminal contribution to the hypertext systems. Only 2,000 softcover copies were printed, and 100 hardcover, numbered and signed by Doug Engelbart and Tim Berners-Lee. 30 pages, 5.5″×9″ includes Epilogue and details of the Award. Engelbart's book is now being republished by the Doug Engelbart Institute.[35]

Two comprehensive histories of Engelbart's laboratory and work are in *What the Dormouse Said: How the Sixties Counterculture Shaped the Personal Computer Industry* by John Markoff and *A Heritage of Innovation: SRI's First Half Century*[36] by Donald Neilson. Other books on Engelbart and his laboratory include *Bootstrapping: Douglas Engelbart, Coevolution, and the Origins of Personal Computing* by Thierry Bardini and *The Engelbart Hypothesis: Dialogs with Douglas Engelbart*, by Valerie Landau and Eileen Clegg in conversation with Douglas Engelbart.[37] All four of these books are based on interviews with Engelbart as well as other contributors in his laboratory.

Engelbart is now Founder Emeritus of the Doug Engelbart Institute, which he founded in 1988 with his daughter Christina Engelbart, who is now Executive Director. The Institute promotes Engelbart's philosophy for boosting Collective IQ—the concept of dramatically improving how we can solve important problems together—using a strategic *bootstrapping* approach for accelerating our progress toward that goal.[38]

In 2005 Engelbart received a National Science Foundation grant to fund the open source HyperScope [39] project. The Hyperscope team built a browser component using Ajax and DHTML designed to replicate Augment's multiple viewing and jumping capabilities (linking within and across various documents). HyperScope is perceived as the first step of a process designed to engage a wider community in a dialogue, on development of collaborative software and services, based on Engelbart's goals and research. The Doug Engelbart Institute is now based at SRI International.

Engelbart has served on the Advisory Boards of the University of Santa Clara Center for Science, Technology, and Society [40], Foresight Institute,[26] Computer Professionals for Social Responsibility, The Technology Center of Silicon Valley, and The Hyperwords Company Ltd (producer of the Firefox Add-On called Hyperwords.[41]

Family

Engelbart has four children, Gerda, Diana, Christina and Norman with his first wife of 47 years, Ballard who died in 1997. He has nine grandchildren. He remarried on January 26, 2008 to writer and producer Karen O'Leary Engelbart.[42] [43] An 85th birthday celebration was held at the Tech Museum of Innovation.[44]

See also

* Dynamic Knowledge Repository
* Collective intelligence

References

[1] http://www.dougengelbart.org/about/dei-footnote.html
[2] http://dougengelbart.org
[3] http://www.computerhistory.org/fellowawards/index.php?id=45
[4] BBC News Online: *The Man behind the Mouse* (http://news.bbc.co.uk/hi/english/sci/tech/newsid_1633000/1633972.stm)
[5] *The Unfinished Revolution II: Strategy and Means for Coping with Complex Problems* (http://www.dougengelbart.org/colloquium/ colloquium.html), Colloquium at Stanford University, Jan–Mar 2000.
[6] About a Bootstrapping Strategy (http://www.dougengelbart.org/about/bootstrapping-strategy.html) — an introduction with links to source materials.
[7] Lowood, Henry (Dec. 19, 1986): *Douglas Engelbart Interview 1* (http://www-sul.stanford.edu/depts/hasrg/histsci/ssvoral/engelbart/ main1-ntb.html), Stanford and the Silicon Valley. Oral History Interviews.
[8] Dr. Douglas C. Engelbart. "Curriculum Vitae" (http://dougengelbart.org/about/cv.html). The Doug Engelbart Institute. . Retrieved April 14, 2011.
[9] The computer mouse turns 40 (http://www.macworld.com/article/137400/2008/12/mouse40.html). Retrieved 16 April 2009.
[10] How Doug was influenced by Vannevar Bush's "As We May Think" (http://dougengelbart.org/events/vannevar-bush-symposium. html#2)
[11] Engelbart Patents (http://www.dougengelbart.org/about/patents.html)
[12] Douglas C. Engelbart (October 1962). "Augmenting Human Intellect: A Conceptual Framework" (http://www.dougengelbart.org/pubs/ augment-3906.html). *SRI Summary Report AFOSR-3223*. Prepared for: Director of Information Sciences, Air Force Office of Scientific Research. . Retrieved April 14, 2011.

[13] http://www.google.com/patents?vid=3541541

[14] Engelbart, Douglas C., et al. (1968), "SRI-ARC. A technical session presentation at the Fall Joint Computer Conference in San Francisco, December 9, 1968" (NLS demo '68: The computer mouse debut), 11 film reels and 6 video tapes (100 min.), Engelbart Collection, Stanford University Library, Menlo Park (CA).

[15] JESSICA SAVIO. "Browsing history: A heritage site is being set up in Boelter Hall 3420, the room the first Internet message originated in" (http://www.dailybruin.com/index.php/article/2011/04/browsing_history). *UCLA Daily Bruin.* .

[16] Chris Sutton. "Internet Began 35 Years Ago at UCLA with First Message Ever Sent Between Two Computers" (http://web.archive.org/web/20080308120314/http://www.engineer.ucla.edu/stories/2004/Internet35.htm). *UCLA.* Archived from the original (http://www.engineer.ucla.edu/stories/2004/Internet35.htm) on 2008-03-08. .

[17] "Elizabeth J. Feinler" (http://alumni.sri.com/hofbios/Elizabeth J.Feinler 2000.htm). *SRI Alumni Hall of Fame.* 2000. . Retrieved April 8, 2011.

[18] Thierry Bardini; Michael Friedewald (2002). "Chronicle of the Death of a Laboratory: Douglas Engelbart and the Failure of the Knowledge Workshop" (http://www.friedewald-family.de/Publikationen/HoT2002.pdf). *History of Technology* **23**: 192–212. .

[19] *About an Open Hyperdocument System* (http://dougengelbart.org/about/ohs.html) an introduction with links to Doug's key writings on the subject

[20] *Honors Awarded to Doug Engelbart* (http://www.dougengelbart.org/about/honors.html)

[21] http://svarchive.stanford.edu/

[22] http://unrev.stanford.edu/

[23] http://dougengelbart.org/colloquium/colloquium.html

[24] http://scpd.stanford.edu/engelbart_colloquium/index.jsp Video archives of 2000 *UnRev-II: Engelbart's Colloquium at Stanford*

[25] Video rchives of 1998 *"Engelbart's Unfinished Revolution" Symposium* (http://scpd.stanford.edu/engelbart_colloquium/index.jsp#EngelbartsUnfinishedRevolution)

[26] "Douglas Engelbart, Foresight Advisor, Is Awarded National Medal of Technology". *Foresight Update* (Foresight Institute) **43**. December 30, 2000.

[27] http://www.pbs.org/cringely/nerdtv/shows/

[28] Engelbart and the Dawn of Interactive Computing (http://www.sri.com/engelbart-event.html)

[29] The Doug Engelbart Institute (http://dougengelbart.org/)

[30] NMC Fellow award (http://www.nmc.org/2009-summer-conference)

[31] Error: Bad DOI specified!

[32] "IEEE Computer Society Magazine Honors Artificial Intelligence Leaders" (http://www.digitaljournal.com/pr/399442). *DigitalJournal.com.* August 24, 2011. . Retrieved September 18, 2011. Press release source: *PRWeb* (Vocus).

[33] Program for the Future

[34] Engelbart Books (http://www.dougengelbart.org/library/books.html)

[35] The Doug Engelbart Institute (http://www.dougengelbart.org/)

[36] http://www.sri.com/about/history/nielson_book.html

[37] "The Engelbart Hypothesis: Dialogs with Douglas Engelbart"

[38] Doug's Vision Highlights: *Augmenting Society's Collective IQ* (http://www.dougengelbart.org/about/vision-highlights.html)

[39] http://hyperscope.org

[40] http://www.scu.edu/sts/

[41] http://www.hyperwords.net/about_us_adv.html

[42] "Celebrating Doug's 85th Birthday" (http://dougengelbart.org/events/celebrating-dougs-85th-birthday.html). Doug Engelbart Institute. . Retrieved April 14, 2011.

[43] "Karen O'Leary, Palo Alto, Writer and Producer" (http://karenengelbart.com/). Karen O'Leary Englebart. . Retrieved April 14, 2011.

[44] "Legends and Beginners of Science". *San Jose Mercury News.* January 31, 2010.

Further reading

- Bardini, Thierry (2000). *Bootstrapping: Douglas Engelbart, Coevolution, and the Origins of Personal Computing*. Stanford: Stanford University Press. ISBN 0804737231.
- Landau, Valerie; Clegg, Eileen (2009). *The Engelbart Hypothesis: Dialogs with Douglas Engelbart* (http:// engelbartbook.com). Berkeley: Next Press.

External links

🔊 **External audio**
Audio
🔊 "Collective IQ and Human Augmentation" (http://www.stranova.com/Podcasts/Stranova28.mp3), Interview with Douglas Engelbart
Videos
🎞 Doug Engelbart featured on JCN Profiles (http://www.archive.org/details/XD304_95JCNProfile), Archive.org

- Doug Engelbart's official website and home of the Doug Engelbart Institute (http://dougengelbart.org/) (formerly Bootstrap)
- Engelbart course facilitated by Valerie Landau at CSU Monterey Bay (http://www.roundworldmedia.com/ engelbart.html)
- U.C. Berkeley Lecture in IEOR 190C (http://www.youtube.com/watch?v=oBZXfCw7xIw) Feb. 2008
- Douglas C. Engelbart Papers, 1953-2005 (http://www.oac.cdlib.org/findaid/ark:/13030/ft3n39n626)(call number M0638; 464 linear ft.) are housed in the Department of Special Collections and University Archives (http://library.stanford.edu/depts/spc/spc.html) at Stanford University Libraries (http://library.stanford.edu/)
- *Engelbart's Unfinished Revolution* (http://unrev.stanford.edu/); December 1998 at Stanford University
- Engelbart and the Dawn of Interactive Computing (http://www.sri.com/engelbart-event.html) — December 9, 2008 — 40th anniversary commemorative event
- The History of Doug Engelbart and Interactive Computing (http://invisiblerevolution.net)
- As We May Work — the Pursuit of Collective IQ (http://www.almaden.ibm.com/coevolution/bio/index. shtml?engelbart), from IBM Symposium site
- Wired article: The Click Heard Round The World (http://www.wired.com/wired/archive/12.01/mouse_pr. html)
- Transcript (http://switch.sjsu.edu/nextswitch/categories/issue18/invitational/switch_engelbart_transcript. pdf) of 2003 visit to San Jose State University (http://cadre.sjsu.edu)
- *Doug Engelbart: Father of the Mouse* (http://www.superkids.com/aweb/pages/features/mouse/mouse.html)
- *Doug Engelbart 1968 Demo* (http://sloan.stanford.edu/MouseSite/1968Demo.html) Original 90-minute video from MouseSite (http://sloan.stanford.edu/MouseSite/)
- OpenAugment Consortium (http://www.openaugment.org/), dedicated to the preservation of the Augment system
- SRI mouse (http://www.sri.com/about/timeline/mouse.html)
- Doug Engelbart Video Archives (http://www.archive.org/details/dougengelbartarchives), Archive.org

Article Sources and Contributors

Computer_Professionals_for_Social_Responsibility *Source*: http://en.wikipedia.org/w/index.php?title=Computer_Professionals_for_Social_Responsibility *Contributors*: AaronSw, AutumnSnow, Carabinieri, Dougschuler, Egil, Horow021, Lquilter, Malcolma, Mephistophelian, PKT, Pearle, Pegship, Robertvan1, Ryan2845, SuperDude115, Thom2729, Torla42, Trbdavies, WBardwin, Widefox, Zodon, Zr2d2, 15 anonymous edits

Electronic_Privacy_Information_Center *Source*: http://en.wikipedia.org/w/index.php?title=Electronic_Privacy_Information_Center *Contributors*: Andy Marchbanks, Blankfaze, Brewcrewer, Chester Markel, Couch on his Head and Smiling, Cybercobra, DMCer, ESkog, Edward, Epeefleche, Fatespeaks, Gaius Cornelius, Joseph Solis in Australia, Linusthefish, Lquilter, Lzur, Petersam, Phil Boswell, R'n'B, Redhanker, Remuel, Rjwilmsi, Salamurai, Stevertigo, Udzu, User36, Vgranucci, Volt4ire, ZimZalaBim, Zodon, 22 anonymous edits

Computers,_Freedom_and_Privacy_Conference *Source*: http://en.wikipedia.org/w/index.php?title=Computers%2C_Freedom_and_Privacy_Conference *Contributors*: Chl, Dawynn, Discospinster, Edward, Glogger, GrahamHardy, Kai-Hendrik, Lcoiney111, Lquilter, Pegship, PotentialDanger, Samuel Blanning, SimonLyall, Sj, Stuartyeates, Zundark, 10 anonymous edits

PARC_(company) *Source*: http://en.wikipedia.org/w/index.php?title=PARC_%28company%29 *Contributors*: -Majestic-, 165.91.209.xxx, 16@r, 7265, Ahoerstemeier, Al Lemos, Alan Millar, Alpha Quadrant, AndroidCat, Aphilo, Aymanshamma, Bernhard.kaindl, BitterMan, Broadacre, C S, Calbaer, Cander0000, Charles Matthews, ClarkCT, Clicketyclack, Conversion script, Coolcaesar, Comellrockey, Crazyhistory, CyberSkull, Cybercobra, DXBari, DanielWeinreb, Dark droid, Davechatting, David Eppstein, Dawnseeker2000, Debuzna, Deodar, Dezirik2795, Disavian, Donfbreed, Drivinghighway61, Dyl, Ecwaine, Ed Poor, Elano, Enviroboy, Evil saltine, Fedallah, Fleminra, Forlornturtle, FrenchIsAwesome, Fryn, Gazpacho, George100, Ggoddard, Gnebulon, Gobonobo, Graham87, Harald Haugland, Harej, Hede2000, Hervegirod, Hirzel, Hooperbloob, IMSoP, Immunize, Ivan Štambuk, Ixfd64, Jakuzem, JamesBWatson, Jermantowicz, Jerryobject, Jim Horning, Jim.henderson, Jim10701, Jmchuff, Jnc, JohnSawyer, Kbdank71, Kdau, Kinema, Kowloonese, Kross, LockeShocke, MarkRichardBeaulieu, Markbeaulieu, Martha6981, Matt Crypto, MaxH75, Mazzy, Mdd, Mountain, Mschlindwein, Nlaporte, Olivier, OllieFury, Omegatron, PacoWP, Paul Drye, Pdc2010, Piolinfax, Pklose, Prof256, Pzavon, RadRafe, Ramckay, Rcawsey, Red, RedWolf, Ricky81682, SD6-Agent, SDC, SamB, Samuel Blanning, Shogun01, Sietse Snel, Stevenmitchell, Sven nestle3, Takometer, Tempshill, Thalia42, The Nut, They call me Mr. Pibb, Thom2729, Thumperward, Tikiwont, Toresbe, Torla42, Txomin, Ventura, Verloren, Vespristiano, Visik, W Nowicki, Wackymacs, Wasbeer, WhisperToMe, WikiLaurent, Wikid77, Wikiuser100, Windsamurai, XMattingly, Ynlrc, Zeerak88, 141 anonymous edits

Strategic_Computing_Initiative *Source*: http://en.wikipedia.org/w/index.php?title=Strategic_Computing_Initiative *Contributors*: CharlesGillingham, Eubulides, Matttoothman, PhnomPencil

Artificial_intelligence *Source*: http://en.wikipedia.org/w/index.php?title=Artificial_intelligence *Contributors*: 100110100, 132.204.25.xxx, 172.141.188.xxx, 17Drew, 1dragon, 200.191.188.xxx, A157247, AAAAA, APH, APL, ARC Gritt, AVBAI, AVGavrilov, Abdullahazzam, Abeg92, Academic Challenger, Acerperi, Acroterion, AdSR, Adam Roush, Adamreiswig, AdjustShift, AdultSwim, AgadaUrbanit, Agemoi, AgnosticPreachersKid, Ahoerstemeier, Ai24081983, Aitias, AlGreen00, Alan Rockefeller, Alansohn, Aldux, Alex naish, Alexf, AlistairMcMillan, Allstarecho, Aloisdimpflmoser, Alsandro, Amareshjoshi, AmiDaniel, Andre Engels, AndrewHZ, Andreworkney, Andy Dingley, Andy Marchbanks, Angr, Aniu, Ankank, Anniepoo, Annonnimus, Antandrus, Anthony Appleyard, Anville, ArielGold, Arne Heise, Arthena, Arthur Rubin, Arthur Smart, ArthurWeasley, ArtificioSapiens, Arvindn, Asbestos, Ashish krazzy, Astrobase36, Atamyrat, Avenged Eightfold, Avery.mabojie, AxelBoldt, Axl, Axon, Aykantspel, AzaToth, Azlan Iqbal, B3virq3b, Baby16, Banes, Banus, Barnaby dawson, BarryList, Basploeger, Bbewsdirector, Beland, Ben Ben, Bender235, Benpryde, Bensin, BertSeghers, Beta Trom, Betacommand, Betterusername, Bforte, Bill52270, Bissinger, Bitsmart, Bjklein, Blackshadow153, Bo Jacoby, Bobblewik, Bobby D. Bryant, Bobianite, Bobo192, Boing! said Zebedee, Boneheadmx, Bongwarrior, Bootedcat, Bootstoots, Borislav, Bornslippy, Bovlb, Bqdemon, Bradgib, Brentdax, Brianjfox, BrightBlackHeaven, Brion VIBBER, BrokenSegue, Brookeweiner, Bryan Derksen, Bryan Seecrets, Bubba2323, Bugone, Burto88, Burzmali, Bustter, CO, COMPFUNK2, CRGreathouse, CWenger, Cabiria, Cacuija, Caiaffa, Can't sleep, clown will eat me, CanadianLinuxUser, Capricorn42, CarlHewitt, Casia wyq, Casper2k3, Cassianp, Centrx, Ceyockey, ChangChienFu, Chaosdruid, ChaoticLogic, Charles Gaudette, CharlesC, CharlesGillingham, Cheesefondue, Chessmaniac, Chicarelli, Chocolateboy, Chopchopwhitey, Chris Roy, Chris.urs-o, Chuckino, Chucks91, Chun-hian, Chuq, Ck lostsword, ClaretAsh, Clarityfiend, Coasterlover1994, Cobratom, Coder Dan, CoderGnome, Coffee2theorems, ColinMcMillen, CommodiCast, ConceptExp, Condem, Conskeptical, Conversion script, Coolcatfish, Corpx, CosineKitty, Cremepuff222, Crunchy Numbers, Csörföly D, Curious1i, Curly Turkey, Cvdwalt, CygnusPius, D, D Monack, DARTH SIDIOUS 2, DHN, DVD R W, Damiens.rf, DanMS, Daniel, DanielDemaret, Danim, Daphne A, Dar-Ape, DarkGhost08, Darker Dreams, Darth Chyrsaor, Darth Panda, Darthali, Davespice, Davewild, David D., David Martland, David.Monniaux, DavidBourguignon, DavidCary, Dcoetzee, Ddxc, DeStilaDo, Dee Jay Randall, Dejitarob, Denisarona, DerHexer, Derek Ross, Dessimoz, Devantheryv, Devonmann101, Dheer7c, Dicklyon, Digsdirt, Diogeneselcinico42, Dionyseus, Dirkbb, Disavian, Discordant, Discospinster, Dispenser, Diza, Dlloader, Dlohcierekim, Dmcq, Dmsar, Docu, DonSiano, DonutGuy, DouglasGreen, Dougofborg, DougsTech, Dpbsmith, Dpupek, Dream land2080, Drift chambers, Drmies, Dublinclontarf, Dudesleeper, Dv82matt, Dysprosia, E prosser, ELApro, ELDRAS, ENeville, EPIC MASTER, ERcheck, ESkog, Eastlaw, EdH, Edgar181, Edivorce, Edward, Eggman64, EisenKnoechel, El C, El aprendelenguas, Elassint, Ellmist, Ellywa, Elsendero, Eluchil, Emarus, Emir Arven, Emperorbma, Emptymountains, Emurph, Emuzesto, Eoghan, Epbr123, Erayman64, Eric Mathews Technology, Eroark, Escientist, Eubulides, Eumolpo, EvanProdromou, Evanh2008, Evanherk, EvelinaB, Evercat, Everyking, Excirial, Eyrian, Eyu100, Ezavarei, Falcon8765, FalconL, Farmer21, Farquaadhnchnm, Fartherred, Fillepa, Finetooth, Finn-Zoltan, Fireboy3015, Flewis, Floquenbeam, Fluffernutter, Foryourinfo, Francob, Francs2000, FrankCostanza, Frans Fowler, Frans-w1, Fraziergeorge122, Frecklefoot, Freek Verkerk, Freemarket, Fribbler, Fricanod, Funandtrvl, Furrykef, Fuzheado, Fvw, GTof, Gabbe, Gadfium, Gaius Cornelius, Galoubet, Gamkiller, Garas, Gary King, Gdm, Gene s, Gengiskanhg, Geoinline, GerryWolff, Giftlite, Gilliam, Gimmetrow, Glacialfox, Glane23, Glen Pepicelli, Glenfarclas, Gmaxwell, Gnome de plume, Gogarburn, Gogo Dodo, Goodnightmush, GraemeL, Grafen, Graham87, Graymornings, GreenReaper, Greensburger, Gregbard, Gregman2, GreyCat, Gridlinked, Grokmoo, Grunt, Guanaco, Guoguo12, Gurch, Gustavo1255, Gwernol, Gyrofrog, Gzabers, Habstinat, Hadal, Halmstad, HamburgerRadio, Hamster Sandwich., Harderm, Harmil, Harriv, Harryboyles, Haseo9999, Haymaker, Healeyb, Heldrain, Herbee, HereToHelp, Heron, Herschelkrustofsky, Hervegirod, Hezarfenn, Hfastedge, Hgamboa, Hi878, Hike395, Horris, Hpdl, Hhth, Hu, Hu12, Hulagutten, Humanrobo, Hydrargyrum, Hydrogen Iodide, I already forgot, IRP, IYY, IanElmore, Iceworks, Ignatzmice, Igoldste, Ihavenolife, Ilcmuchas, ImGz, Implements, Imran, Indyfitz, Inego, Insomniak, IntellectToday, Interested, Intrealm, Introgressive, Inwind, Iohannes Animosus, Ioverka, IrishStephen, Isheden, ItsZippy, Ivant, Ixfd64, Iyerakshay, J. Spencer, J.delanoy, J04n, JCAILLAT, JRR Trollkien, Jackol, Jagdeepyadav, Jagginess, Jaibe, Jake11, James childs, Jamyskis, Jan eissfeldt, Jarble, Jared555, Jason Palpatine, Java7837, Javidjamae, Javierito92, Jayjg, Jdzarlino, Jebba, Jeeny, JesseHogan, Jimothytrotter, Jj137, Jkaplan, JoeSmack, Joeblakesley, Jogers, Johannes Simon, John Newbury, John Vandenberg, John of Reading, JohnOwens, Johnkoza1992, Johnuniq, Jojit fb, Jon Awbrey, Jonathan Métillon, Jonrgrover, Jordan123, Jorfer, Joseph Solis in Australia, Josephorourke, Joydurgin, Jpbowen, Jpgordon, Jroudh, Jrtayloriv, Jsun027, Judson, Julian Mendez, JuniorMonkey, Jvoegele, Jwoodger, K.Nevelsteen, KF, Kaldosh, Kane5187, Karada, KarenEdda, Karol Langner, KellyCoinGuy, Kevin143, Kevyn, Khalid, Khaydarian, Kimveale, King of Hearts, Kingboyk, Kjellmikal, Klafubra, Kneiphof, Koavf, Kostisl, Koyaanis Qatsi, Kramlovesmovies, Kri, Kukini, Kurowoofwoof111, Kzollman, L Kensington, LFaraone, Lacatosias, Larry laptop, LaserBeams, Lateg, LauriO, Laurusnobilis, Lectonar, LedgendGamer, Lee Daniel Crocker, Leire Sánchez, Lenehey, LeoNomis, Leoneris, Leontolstoy2, Leszek Jańczuk, Levineps, Lewblack, Lexor, Libcub, Liftarn, Liger, Lightmouse, Lilac Soul, Lilinjing cas, Linweizhen, LittleBenW, Livajo, Logperson, Loki en, Looxix, Loremaster, Loxley, Lumos3, Luna Santin, Lylodo, Lynn Wilbur, M, MCTales, MD87, MER-C, MHLU, MIT Trekkie, MJBurrage, MTuffield, Mac, Mac-steele, MacMed, Macduffman, Macilnar, MadSurgeon, Madd4Max, Maghnus, Mailseth, MakeRocketGoNow, Malignedtruth, MangoWong, Mani1, Marc Girod, Marc Venot, Marek69, MarkAb, Marktindal, Markus.Waibel, Martha2000, Martinp, Marudubshinki, Marysunshine, Master Jaken, MasterOfHisOwnDomain, MattBan, Matteh, Matthew Stannard, Maureen, Mausy5043, Mav, Maver1ck, Maximus Rex, Mayfly may fly, McCart42, McGeddon, Mdd, Mdebets, Me pras, MeekMark, Melody, Memming, Mendel, Mercury, Metamagician3000, MiNombreDeGuerra, Micahmn, Michael Fourman, Michael Hardy, Michal Jurosz, MichalJurosz, Mikael Häggström, Mike Schwartz, MikeCapone, MikeLynch, Mild Bill Hiccup, MilesMi, Mindmatrix, Minesweeper, Mintguy, Mmernex, Mmxx, Mneser, Monkee13, Moralis, Mostlymark, Moxon, Mr.Sisgay, MrJones, MrOllie, Mrsolutions, Mrvasin, Mschel, Mschures, Mudd1, Mullhawk, Muness, Myanw, Myasuda, Myncknm, NCurse, Nabarry, Nabeth, NachOking, Nanshu, Naohiro19, NapoleonB, Nappy1020, Nayanraut, Ndenison, Neckelmann, NeilN, Neilc, Neko-chan, Netesq, Neverquick, Newkidd11, Nick, Nickj, Nightscream, Nishkid64, Nistra, Nixdorf, Noctibus, Nondescript, Normxxx, NorrYtt, Novum, Nposs, Nuclear Treason, NuclearWarfare, Nufy8, Nunocordeiro, Nx7000, Obscuranym, Ohconfucius, Olathe, Oldhamlet, Oleg Alexandrov, Olethros, Olinga, Oliver Pereira, Olivier, Olof nord, Onorem, Opelio, Orangemike, Ost316, Ott, OwenX, Owlbuster, Oxwil, Oxymoron83, Pacas, Palace of the Purple Emperor, Paradoctor, Paul A, Pawyilee, Pegua, Peterdjones, PetroKonashevich, Peyre, Pgr94, Phileas, Philip Trueman, Piet Delport, Pigsonthewing, Pilotguy, Pinethicket, Piotrus, Pjoef, Pkirlin, Pluke, PluniAlmoni, Poccil, Poiman, Pokrajac, Polocrunch, Poor Yorick, Pooya.babahajyani, Populus, Prakashavinash, Pravdaverita, Preslethe, Prohlep, Prolog, PrometheusX303, Psb777, Pspoulin, Psych2012Joordens, Psychonaut, Public Menace, Pud button, Qartis, Qswitch426, Qwertyus, R. S. Shaw, RCPayne, RJASE1, RK, RabidDeity, Rafael.perez.rosario, Rahuldharmani, Rajah, Ralf Klinkenberg, Rangoon11, Ranjithsutari, Rasmus Faber, Ratiocinate, Reckiz, Recognizance, Reconsider the static, RedHillian, RedWolf, Redaktor, Redvers, Reidgsmith, Remember the dot, Remy B, Renaissancee, Renamed user 3, Rene halle, Rettetast, RexNL, Rgarvage, Rhobite, Rholton, Riccardopoli, Rich Farmbrough, Richard001, Richardcavell, Rick Block, Ricvelozo, Rinea, Ripe, Risk one, Rjwilmsi, Rlw, Rnb, Robert Merkel, Robin klein, Roesslerj, Ronz, Rootxploit, Rpmorrow, Rror, Rumping, Ruslik0, Ruud Koot, RyanParis, Ryguasu, Rzwitserloot, S0aasdf2sf, SDC, SWAdair, Sagaciousuk, Saizai, Salamurai, Sam Hocevar, Sam Korn, Sander123, Sango123, Sarnholm, Sbennett4, Sceptre, Schaefer, Schlegel, SchreyP, Science History, Scorpion451, Sdornan, SeanMack, Seaphoto, Searchmaven, Searchme, Seb az86556, Sebaldusadam, Sebastian scha., SecretStory, Selket, Sgunteratparamus.k12.nj.us, Shadow1, Shadowjams, Shaggorama, Shanes, Shannonbonannon, Shanoman, Shenme, Shirik, Shpiget, Shuipzv3, Siddharthsk2000, Sillybilly, Simbara, Simoneau, Sirkad, Smallclone2, SnoopY, Snoutholder, Snoyes, SocratesJedi, Sodium, Sole Soul, SouthernNights, Sparkygravity, Special-T, Spinningobo, Spitfire, Srinivasasha, Staberind, Stardust8212, Stefanomione, SteinbDJ, Stephane.magnenat, Stephen G Graham, StephenReed, Stevage, Steve Quinn, Stevertigo, Stoni, Stormie, Stroppolo, Supten, Susvolans, Svick, Sweetness46, Symane, Syncategoremata, Syrthiss, Szeldich, TAnthony, THEN WHO WAS PHONE?, Tabortiger, Taemyr, Taggart Transcontinental, Tailpig, Talon Artaine, Tarotcards, Tassedethe, Taw, Taxisfolder, Taylormas229, Tazmaniacs, Tdewey, Technopat, Tedickey, Teo64x, ThG, The Anome, The Cunctator, The Divine Fluffalizer, The Evil IP address, The Magnificent Clean-keeper, The Thing That Should Not Be, The Transhumanist (AWB), The world deserves the truth, The wub, TheDoober, TheRanger, TheSix, Thecheesykid, Thede, Themfromspace, Theo Pardilla, Theropod-X, Theyer, Thiseye, Thomas Kist, Thumperward, Thunderhippo, Thüringer, Tiddly Tom, Tideflat, Tillander, Time for action, Timwi, Titus III, Tkinias, Tkorrovi, Tobias Bergemann, Tobias Kuhn, Toby Bartels, Tokek, Tommy Herbert, Tone, Tony1, Took, Topazxx, Touisiau, Tpbradbury, Tremilux, Trevor MacInnis, Truthnlove, Turk oğlan, TurntableX, TutterMouse, Twexcom, TwoOneTwo, Tzartzam, Ugen64, Una Smith, Uncle Dick, Unknown, Unreal7, Urod, Useight, Utcursch, VSimonian, Varagrawal, Velho, Vesal, Vespine, Vfrias, Vidstige, Vilerage, Virtualerian, Viskonsas, Vivohobson, Voices cray, Vrenator, Vrossi1, Vsmith, WBtheFROG, WMod-NS, Wadeduck, Wafulz, Walter Fritz, Wasell, WaveRunner85, Wavelength, Wdfarmer, WereSpielChequers, Wesleymurphy, Westwood25, Wfructose, WhatisFeelings?,

Wiki alf, Wiki-uoft, WikiNing, Wikicolleen, Wikiklrsc, Wikireviewer99, Wikiwikifast, Wile E. Heresiarch, William conway bcc, Witbrock, Wizardist, Wmahan, WojPob, Wookiee cheese, Wyckster, Wyklety, Xensyria, Xklsv, Xobritbabeox10, Xzbobzx, Yakota21, Yankee-Bravo, Yardcock, Ykalyan, YoungFreud, Yoyosocool, Ypetrachenko, Yuckfoo, Yungjibbz, ZENDELBACH, Zaklog, Zapvet, ZeroOne, Zntrip, Zsinj, Zubenelgenubi, Zundark, Zzthex, Zzuuzz, ²¹², Ásgeir IV., Δ, Иъ Лю Ха, 2022 anonymous edits

Community_network *Source*: http://en.wikipedia.org/w/index.php?title=Community_network *Contributors*: Buffty, Calltech, Careyoconnor, Chaosdruid, Charles Matthews, Chowbok, Cmdrjameson, DanMS, Edward, Gregoryclarke, Ikusawa, Joseph Solis in Australia, Lukobe, Mikemoral, Philippe, Samvao2, Samvaro2, Shahhhn, Sjjupadhyay, Sungirl48, Tomos, 17 anonymous edits

Communications of the ACM *Source*: http://en.wikipedia.org/w/index.php?title=Communications_of_the_ACM *Contributors*: Adnaddriegw, AlexPlank, Allen3, Altenmann, Andyjsmith, BD2412, Bencherlite, Corsarius, D3, Deodar, Dsp13, Gingekerr, Guillaume2303, Headbomb, Hermel, Ilario, Innotata, Jpbowen, Lambiam, MCiura, Mikeblas, Miym, Naif Alsharabi, Neilc, Pearle, Pernambuco, Piano non troppo, Quatloo, Qwertyus, R'n'B, Robert Merkel, Schneelocke, SimonP, Softy, Suruena, Tohd8BohaithuGh1, TomT0m, Vicki Rosenzweig, Wernher, Xasodfuih, 14 anonymous edits

Barbara_Simons *Source*: http://en.wikipedia.org/w/index.php?title=Barbara_Simons *Contributors*: Bbsimons, DMCer, Deville, Douglas W. Jones, Dsp13, Edward, Electiontechnology, Esmito, JLaTondre, Jiang, Jmabel, June w, Ketiltrout, Levineps, R'n'B, SimonP, Thayvian, Topbanana, Truthteller11, 10 anonymous edits

Douglas_Engelbart *Source*: http://en.wikipedia.org/w/index.php?title=Douglas_Engelbart *Contributors*: =ppy, Aboutmovies, Adib5271, Admrboltz, Ajbenj, Al Lemos, Alan Millar, Alansohn, Alison, Alma Pater, Andrei Stroe, AndrewHowse, Andrwsc, Aristotle, Arminius, Arthena, Asiananimal, AxelBoldt, BSveen, Backslash Forwardslash, Beaucouplusneutre, Bender235, Berkeley@gmail.com, Betacommand, Bevo, Blanchardb, Blogjack, Bobber100, Bobblewik, BradBRR, Brandon, Braphael, CWii, CanisRufus, Capricorn42, Carlos T. Blackburn, Cayzle, Cengelbart, Cflm001, Chaiken, Chapter8, Charles Matthews, Chase me ladies, I'm the Cavalry, Classicfilms, Cnilep, CommonsDelinker, Computerhistory, Conversion script, Coolcaesar, Copysan, CrabCakesX, Css, Cyanoa Crylate, D6, DXBari, Dakart, Dalliance, Darth Panda, DavidWBrooks, Decltype, Dengelbart, Deodar, Derek Ross, Diego Moya, Dispenser, Dolovis, DougEngland, Dougengelbart, Dr.K., Dysepsion, Dysprosia, Dzag, Edward, Egil, Eileenclegg, Elliskev, Eloquence, Engeleary, Engology, Eranb, Eras-mus, Eric Shalov, Eumolpo, Excirial, Facius, Flora Cozzi, Fraudy, Frecklefoot, Gaius Cornelius, Garion96, Gcampbel, Giftlite, Gilliam, Gorgalore, Graham87, Greatestrowerever, Grlloyd, Gwernol, Hephaestos, Herostratus, Husky, I5bala, Ian Burnet, Ian Pitchford, Imagine123456789, J.delanoy, JTN, Jamesmorrison, Jatkins, Jeepday, Jeff G., Jeromealden85, Jerryobject, Jessemerriman, Jfrulifson, Jimbo Wales, Jmabel, Jni, John Vandenberg, Johnny99, JonHarder, Jpbowen, Jrcla2, KYPark, KarenEngelbart, Kbdank71, Kitsune361, Kku, Kosmopolis, Kurykh, Kushal one, Lampica, Lemeza Kosugi, Li4kata, LilHelpa, Liquidizer, LockeShocke, M3tainfo, MER-C, MLFungwiki, Maniadis, Marcelo1229, Marcerickson, MarcoTolo, MarkSweep, Martarius, Matt Crypto, Mav, Mdebruijn, Memex, Mereda, Michael Devore, Midinastasurazz, MikeVitale, Minesweeper, Moulder, Moverton, Mpbarbosa, Mr Stephen, MrVibrating, Mrmatiko, Mschel, Mugunth Kumar, N0YKG, N328KF, NawlinWiki, Nfm, Nightscream, Nima Baghaei, Norm mit, Nsaa, Nv8200p, Ohconfucius, Opablo, Ottawahitech, Owen, Paul.h, Pavel Vozenilek, Peak, Pemboid, Perey, Peteforsyth, Pgan002, Pipedreamergrey, Playaoms11, Polylerus, PsychoSmith, RFerreira, RJBurkhart3, Rakscyn, Resurgent insurgent, Rich Farmbrough, Richard Arthur Norton (1958-), RichardVeryard, Ricky81682, Riddley, Rj, Rl, Robert K S, Robert Merkel, Roberta F., Rodrigo braz, RoyBoy, Rsabbatini, Ryan Postlethwaite, Sakhalinrf, SallyForth123, Sashazlv, Scarian, SchreyP, Sdornan, Smallman12q, Somerwind, Sprachpfleger, SqueakBox, Sstruce, StaticGull, Sulair.speccoll, Supergee, Suruena, Suryadas, SusanLesch, Thief12, Threner, Thumperward, Thüringer, Tkynerd, Tom-, Treekids, Triona, Trontonic, Truthnlove, TuukkaH, Vanished User 0001, Vdgr, VegaDark, Viriditas, Vlandau@gmail.com, W Nowicki, W163, Wanderingstan, Wereon, WernerPopken, Wernher, Wgungfu, Wikidemon, Wikiklrsc, Wikkrockiana, Wiknerd, Winchelsea, Yahoo, Zoicon5, 378 anonymous edits

Image Sources, Licenses and Contributors

Printed by Books on Demand GmbH, Norderstedt / Germany